RUNNING FITNESS

David Ross

Grosvenor House
Publishing Limited

This book is published by
Grosvenor House Publishing Ltd
28-30 High Street, Guildford, Surrey, GU1 3EL.
www.grosvenorhousepublishing.co.uk

A CIP record for this book
is available from the British Library

ISBN 978-1-78148-349-7

Disclaimer

This book contains ideas about exercise, running, stretching, nutrition and energy food consumption that may not be applicable to everyone. You should always consult a medical practitioner if you are concerned with any aspect of your health or have any doubts about your general ability to take up running as a sport. The content of this book is aimed at senior adults over the age of 18 years but is not specific to either men or women or tailored to any specific personal or health requirements. This book contains information that should be used for general purposes only. Nothing should be taken as professional advice or diagnosis. The activities in this book should not be used as a substitute for any treatment or medication prescribed to you by a medical practitioner. The author and publisher do not accept any responsibility for any adverse effects that may occur as a result of the use of the suggestions or information herein. If you feel that you are experiencing any adverse effects after embarking on any health improvement endeavour, including any of the suggestions made in this book, it is important that you seek medical advice. Results from any of the suggestions in this book may vary from individual to individual. The content of this book does not represent any formal or informal statement on behalf of any running organisation or governing body.

To all runners prepared to work hard and achieve something great

- David Ross

Contents

About the author

David Ross started running in 1988 and has a full marathon personal best time of 3:24 (Chicago 2006) and a half marathon personal best of 1:30 (Reading 2010). He is a member of the Datchet Dashers running club in Windsor, Berkshire, a *Leader in Running Fitness* (UK Athletics) and the former race director of the Maidenhead Easter Ten road race (2006-2009).

Acknowledgements

My thanks go to:

- The late Shihan Dominick McCarthy (8th Dan), Founder of Zen Judo, who back in 1988, gave me the chance to grade for black belt. The whole thing inadvertently led me to discover running and all that it had to offer.

- Alex Roslow, for helping with the stretches and core fitness images, and to Jan Frost for her patience and attention to detail in drawing them all.

- Gemma Taylor, for her assistance designing the front cover.

- Ruth Kitching, for her help and contributions in reviewing the manuscript, and not to mention her unstinting friendship over the years.

- Valerie Archibald, for her valuable feedback, plus various other creative inputs that have made all the difference.

- Nina Smith, Michael Hill, Cherry Key, Helen Preedy and Jatindra Rakhra, for their feedback and inputs during the review stages.

- Kim Cross and the team at Grosvenor House Publishing for turning the manuscript into a formal publication.

- My family and close friends for their support and encouragement that I have received.

Enjoy your running practice and I hope that it rewards you.

David P.J. Ross
Maidenhead, Berkshire, UK
January 2015

Running Fitness

From 5K to Full Marathon:

An Overview

Background and introduction

When it comes to everyday exercising, running is a popular and well known way of keeping fit. The basic practice of running comes naturally to most of us, but as we shall see in later chapters, the development of performance and endurance takes time and persistence. Running can be a highly rewarding experience and the current growth in participation looks set to continue well into the future.

I inadvertently stumbled across running back in my late teens and originally came about as a result of preparing for a judo grading. I started to run on a regular basis as a way of improving my general fitness in advance of the grading day; a useful endeavour that would make all the difference. Then having successfully passed the grading, I still carried on running three to four times a week, the main reason being that I just enjoyed it.

I realised very quickly how important regular running had become. Through running training, I had certainly learnt the benefits of cardiovascular and physical strength development – I needed to develop these to survive the judo grading that I mentioned earlier. But as time went by, I also realised how running created an amazing *feel-good* factor. I also felt more alert and sharp as an individual and I still believe that running has enabled me to bring a great deal of energy and enthusiasm to many personal and professional endeavours throughout the years. As time progressed, I also started to lose some weight and trim up a little.

I found getting into running quite an easy thing to do. I simply bought a pair of running shoes and did a short run one evening and then the rest, as they say, was history. Within a six-month period I simply developed my distance from about 1-mile up to around 5 miles. I tended to run three to four times a week, as I still do now on average.

When I first started regular running, I tended to take things quite gently and never got too ambitious during the early stages. I believe that this was one of the main reasons why I have stuck with the sport for so long. There is no doubt that success and longevity in running is about learning how to train within our individual physical and aerobic limits.

Within a few years of becoming a regular runner I started to take part in races, one of the first being the Portsmouth Half Marathon. Racing taught me about the virtues of having goals and something to aim for. As time went by, I would race more often and eventually join a running club. This gave me the opportunity to do *cross country* racing and train for a full marathon; the latter being an endeavour that I would do eleven times in total. I would also start to take part in my local *parkrun* (www.parkrun.com).

In summary, it was aerobic development, more energy for everyday living, enhanced personal wellbeing, the drive to achieve goals, plus the added advantage of being able to maintain a healthy body weight that were the main reasons why I stuck with running and perhaps became a bit of a running addict in the process. These are also very similar reasons as to why many other everyday people regularly take to their shoes – motivation, challenge, a feel-good factor, and for those who enjoy racing, to get faster.

Chapter summaries
Running Fitness From 5K to Full Marathon is written *for* a runner *by* a runner, and is designed to encourage people to practice the sport in a way that promotes enjoyment, success and longevity. There are seven chapters, each covering a discrete part of running.

Chapter 1 is a general and introductory chapter that focuses on health and fitness assessments. Being in good health is an important part of being a runner, and health and fitness tests are a great way of seeing how fit you are and whether or not there are any health issues that may prevent you from enjoying running. The subject of aerobic exercise and weight loss is also touched upon. Many people practice running because they think that it is an easy solution to a weight problem. Unfortunately, these kinds of messages are a tad oversold.

Chapter 2 is primarily aimed at *beginners* to running and introduces combinations of *Power-walking*, *Jogging* and *Easy-paced* running as a structured and effective way of getting started. We will also consider some basic *warm-up* and *cool-down* routines. This is a critical part of ensuring that training sessions are of a quality nature and that we keep injuries down to a minimum.

Chapter 3 is about nutrition and hydration and is split into three parts that look at what we eat and drink and how we fuel our body. *Part I* considers our food diet with a specific focus on protein, fat and the role of carbohydrates in a runners diet. *Part II* looks at the role and purpose of energy supplements like energy drinks and gels. *Part III* discusses fluid intake and hydration and how we can prevent things like dehydration.

Chapter 4 is about the crux of what we do in running training. The chapter starts off by introducing some advanced *warm-up* and *cool-down* stretches that build on the basic stretches that were introduced back in Chapter 2. The main content focuses around the training techniques and practices of *VO2 Max*, *Threshold*, *Hills*, *Long runs*, *Race pace*, *Recovery* and *Rest*. If we want to develop our running performance and endurance then we need to master these different styles of training practice. For VO2 Max, Threshold and Hill training, you will be given *three* levels of training to choose from, with level 1 being more for beginners, and levels 2 and 3 aimed at more experienced runners. When we structure our training in this way, we give ourselves the opportunity to gauge our ideal starting point based on our current fitness level, and have a clear and visible training path that will take us to the next level. Some useful advice on injury management and resolution is provided at the tail end of the chapter.

Chapter 5 looks at the advantages of some of the different types of cross training and core fitness activities that many runners regularly indulge in. Cross training and core fitness activities are great ways of developing a strong and upright posture that is good for developing performance and endurance, and keeping injuries at bay.

Chapter 6 presents a number of example race training schedules designed for developing racing capability from 5K through to 10K and up to half marathon. Many runners enjoy taking part in competitions and so my general recommended approach to racing is about developing speed and distance in stages, and that we should only move to the next distance as and when we are ready to do so. Each of the training schedules incorporates many of the ideas from Chapters 4 and 5, such as *Endurance and stamina*, *Speed*, *Recovery and rest* and *Race pace*. The training schedules will help you understand how to integrate the various training practices into a coherent plan aimed at developing race performance. As you progress through the schedules, you can amend them to reflect what works for you as an individual. At the end of each schedule there are suggestions around how to improve your performance for that distance.

Chapter 7 is focused around full marathon training. Two example marathon training schedules are presented that take a sustained half marathon performance as a basis for developing into the full marathon distance (this chapter is effectively a follow-on from Chapter 6 for any reader who started the book from scratch). Training for a full marathon is very different from training for shorter distances. The best marathon performances tend to come from those who develop their racing capability in a way that is consistent and sustainable. This chapter will discuss the many ins and outs of marathon training and prepare you for what to expect.

How to use this book
This book is aimed at senior men and women over the age of 18 and caters for a wide variety of target audiences, ranging from beginners to established runners as well as those looking to teach the sport. Not all aspects of running are easy to grasp first time around and so you may need to revisit some of the material as you progress.

You should nevertheless be able to start reading the chapters, perhaps write down a few notes and then go out and train.

As you progress through each chapter you will come across a number of training *guidelines*, *best practices* and associated *parameters*, some of which are quantifiable, and others more descriptive. You will need to take a view as to where you are based on your current fitness level (this is quite easy to gauge or work out). Once you know where you are in the parameters, you can begin your training endeavours at a pace and a duration that is sustainable. By taking a structured approach, you will give yourself something to aim for simply because you can easily *forward-read* through the respective chapter and gauge the next level of training expectations. For those readers starting from scratch in Chapters 1 and 2, there is a minimum of at least *3-5 years* of solid training covered in this book. Established runners and those looking to teach the sport will no doubt find plenty of useful information and helpful tips. Nevertheless, this book has been written with four main target audiences in mind. They are as follows:

I. Beginners with little or no previous experience in fitness – If you are new to running and have never previously indulged in much fitness then you should focus on Chapters 1 and 2 as a starting point. Once you have developed your warm-up and cool-down drills and you are happy that you can run at an easy pace for at least 40 minutes to an hour, then you are well placed to look at Chapter 3 and then start to tackle some of the training practices in Chapters 4 and 5. Many of the training practices in these particular chapters may seem a little daunting and elitist. The simple truth is that they are not, and that providing you start your training endeavours at the *Level 1* schedules, and then (in a similar way to any other runner) limit your increases in training distance and intensity by 10% in any week then you should be fine. It is important not to become intimidated by more experienced runners. They themselves would have started out in running in a very similar way. Once you have understood some of the basic ideas around what running is all about then you will be well on your way to success.

If you are interested in racing then Chapter 6 will help you complete your first 5K race and show you a path through to 10K and half marathon (13.1 miles). Chapter 7 is all about full marathon training and is more than a future possibility, provided that you develop your training distance and stamina in a way that is gentle and sustainable.

II. Beginners with previous experience in other sports – If you are new to running but have already achieved a good level of fitness from another sport, then some of the aerobic tests in Chapter 1 might be of interest. Otherwise you could go straight into Chapter 2 and start with some simple jogging and easy-paced intervals. Once you can run for at least 40 minutes to an hour at an easy pace then you are well placed to look at Chapters 3 and onwards.

III. Established runners looking to improve in the sport – If you are an established runner looking to learn more about the sport, or are just looking for ways to improve your performance then Chapters 3, 4 and 5 are the core must-read chapters. You may however also find some of the warm-up and cool-down stretches from Chapter 2 useful. Hopefully, as a result of reading these chapters, you will quickly identify what kind of training(s) you need to work on to achieve your goals. If you are frustrated with your race performances then Chapters 6 and 7 not only provide some useful training schedules and associated guidelines, but also further information on how to *improve* your performance in a particular distance.

IV. Trainee running coaches – The best running coaches are those who offer simple and practical advice that works effectively when applied. Depending on whom you are coaching, and whether they are beginners, club runners or more advanced runners, this book contains many training ideas and schedules that can be used for the purposes of organised training sessions and individual training plans.

The world of running
Running is a solo sport by nature, but that certainly doesn't mean that you have to do all of your training by yourself. If you are

interested in doing the sport with other people then the following options are well worth considering:

I. Running clubs – One way of practicing some of the training ideas in this book is to join a running club. This is by far the most popular way of learning about the sport of running. You will also find other people to run with that are of a similar standard to yourself. Most running clubs will hold at least one weekly speed training session, plus longer runs on a Sunday morning for those training for longer distances. Running clubs have (at least historically) been incorrectly perceived as *elitist*. Indeed, you will find that most clubs have a group of faster runners who will be expected to do wonders for their club's public image, but the reality is that many club members are just social runners who are just out to enjoy themselves and see what they can achieve in the time that they put aside for running. Then there is the social side of running; another world in its own right.

II. Beginners courses – Many running clubs hold beginners courses that are designed to introduce people to the sport of running. These provide people with the opportunity to practice running in the company of others and is a great way of building self-confidence. If you are a little nervous about going out running by yourself on the open roads, then a beginners' course (and perhaps then followed by joining a club) is a great way of removing these kinds of barriers.

III. Training camps – Once you have got started in the sport, there are many organisations that arrange running related sporting holidays. One of the more popular and well known getaways is *warm-weather* training where people will spend a week or so training in a sunny location. There are also seasonal training camps focused around a certain area, like (e.g.) full marathon training. These kinds of events are normally good fun, and like running clubs, you will meet all sorts of likeminded people and pick up a variety of training tips that you probably wouldn't have got had you focused on training solo.

Muscles and muscle groups – Front

The picture below and the one on the next page highlights the main *muscles* and *muscle groups* mentioned throughout this book.

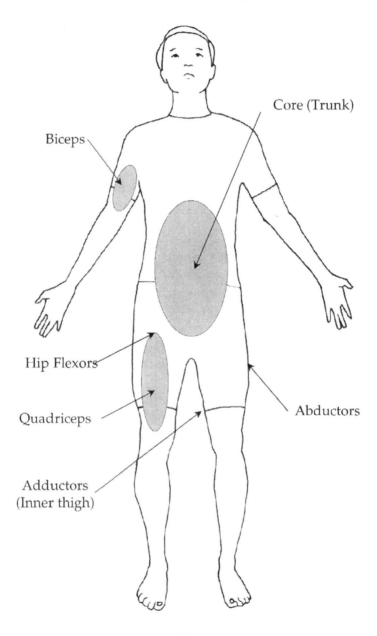

Muscles and muscle groups – Rear

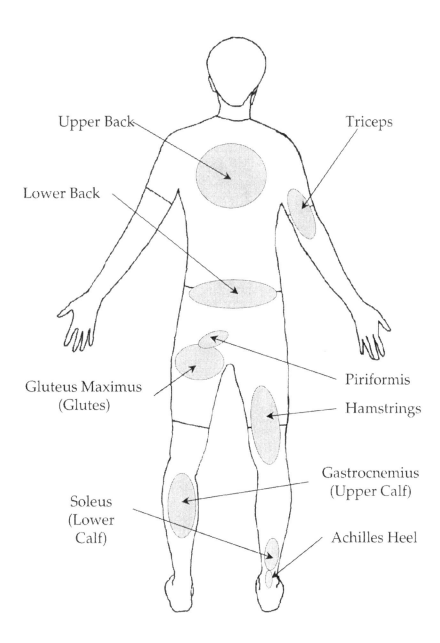

Upper Back

Triceps

Lower Back

Gluteus Maximus
(Glutes)

Piriformis

Hamstrings

Gastrocnemius
(Upper Calf)

Soleus
(Lower
Calf)

Achilles Heel

Chapter 1

Health and Fitness Assessments

Being confident that you are in good health is an important consideration before taking to your shoes. If you are in any doubt about your general health and wellbeing then this chapter presents some useful and highly relevant tests aimed at measuring your individual suitability to running. If, on the other hand, you are already known to be fit and healthy, then there is still no harm in doing a health and fitness assessment just to see how fit you *really* are!

You have a number of options around where you could go for a health and fitness assessment: your local gym or sports clinic are the obvious choices. Another option is to go through your employer or even a Private Health scheme, but you might have to pay.

AN EXAMPLE HEALTH & FITNESS ASSESSMENT

A typical fitness test designed for runners will measure and quantify the following aspects of our general health and aerobic capability:

- Body composition.

- Blood pressure.

- Lung function (Peak Expiratory Flow).

- Aerobic capacity (VO2 Max).

I. Body composition – Excess body fat around the vital organs such as the heart and liver can lead to a variety of life threatening health conditions. For many years, Body Mass Index (BMI) has been used to indicate whether or not someone is *overweight*. BMI is calculated by taking our body weight in kilos and dividing this number by the square value of our height in metres (using *imperial* units, BMI is your body weight in pounds multiplied by 703, divided by the square value of your height in inches). The problem however with BMI is that the formula ignores age, gender, muscle and bone density. This is why *body fat percentage* is considered as a more useful measure. Body fat percentage can be measured using either skin callipers or certain types of electronic bathroom scales.

Category	Women	Men
Essential fat	10–13%	2–5%
Athletes	14–20%	6–13%
Fitness	21–24%	14–17%
Average	25–31%	18–24%
Obese	32%+	25%+

Table 1.1: Typical body fat percentages[1]

Table 1.1 contains some useful guidance as to what our ideal body fat percentages should be. There is no doubt that being a runner will certainly help burn excess body fat, but as we shall see, this will only happen through integrating *what we eat* with *how we train*.

Weight loss can be easily addressed by burning more calories in the form of *fat* than we consume. We can do this in two ways: firstly, by cutting back on processed foods and foods that contain excess carbohydrates, many of which contain high levels of glucose. These kinds of foods stimulate the *creation* of fat cells, a process that happens as a result of surges of *insulin*; a hormone that is responsible for storing fat in the body. To lose weight, our body must use more fat as a source of fuel. When we stop feeding our body with excess glucose, the body will switch to using fat reserves, a process that will ultimately stimulate weight loss. To do this, we should stock up on proteins and fats as a way of fuelling our body as these kinds of foods don't suffer from the fat forming effects of insulin. Many people may have been led to believe that exercise is *the* way to lose weight when actually this is not the whole truth. Foods such as proteins and fats help suppress our appetite and boost our metabolism, another process that will also help burn body fat – more on this in Chapter 3.

The second way of shedding body weight is through taking up an activity like *walking* as a regular form of exercise. For example, a 1-hour walk will consume around 200 calories burned from *fat* metabolism. This is because we burn proportionally *more* calories in the form of fat when we exercise at a *low intensity* (e.g., walking) than we would calories burnt from carbohydrates. The good news is that the structured training plans in Chapter 2 use various combinations of comparatively low intensity aerobic exercise designed to promote fat metabolism as an integral part of becoming a runner. There is no doubt that running increases metabolism and that you will burn more calories as a result, but these need to be *fat* calories for us to lose weight. Carbohydrate consumption only then becomes an important factor for runners who train for longer distances or at higher intensities, something that we will take a closer look at in Chapters 3 and 4.

Carrying an excess amount of body weight when running increases the risk of placing an undue amount of stress on our physical joints and aerobic organs, but this certainly doesn't exclude you from taking up the sport. Once you have begun to follow Chapter 2 and have started to reduce your body fat percentage, then it is likely that you will find running training a far more enjoyable and fulfilling experience.

The correlation between *aerobic exercise* and *weight loss* is discussed in more detail at the end of the chapter.

Dr. John Briffa's book *Escape the diet trap* (www.drbriffa.com) is an excellent and well informed up to date publication for those readers who are interested in broadening their knowledge about general food diet (ISBN 978-0-00-744243-0).

II. Blood pressure – These are the usual standard tests of *systolic pressure* (the higher value) and *diastolic pressure* (the lower value). The recommended systolic and diastolic values for an adult in good health should be between 90 and 120 and 60 and 90, respectively. If your blood pressure values fall within these limits then there shouldn't be any problems. If your blood pressure is either above or below the recommended limits or abnormally high, then a trip to your GP would probably be recommended before taking to the roads.

Generally speaking, people with higher blood pressure caused through smoking, excess body fat and alcohol intake, excess salt in their diet or a general lack of exercise, will be encouraged to follow a more gradual aerobic training programme. This kind of approach will help to strengthen the heart muscles.

III. Lung function – Peak Expiratory Flow (PEF) is a measure of general lung function. A PEF test can gauge how effectively we can take in oxygen, which is then made available for transport by the pumping action of the heart to the muscles. PEF is measured by taking a deep breath and then blowing *out* as hard you can into a peak flow meter.

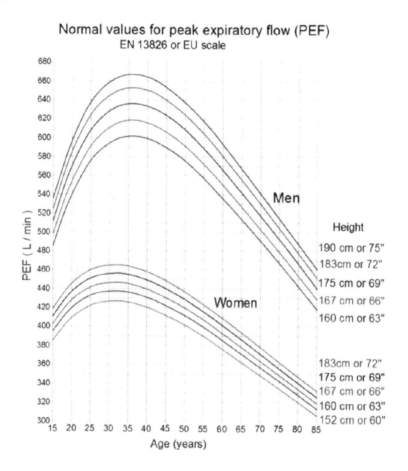

Fig. 1.1: Predicted values for PEF[2]

Our individual PEF will have a direct and noticeable effect on our body's ability to deliver aerobic output. An abnormally low PEF suggests an obstruction or limiting factor in our airways and could point to some kind of lung disorder.

Peak expiratory flow is measured in Litres per Minute. The age and height adapted *EU/EN 13826 scale* in Fig. 1.1 above enables us to gauge our own PEF. For example, a man of 30 years of age with a height of 5'6" should have a PEF of 610 Litres/Minute. A woman of 40 years of age with a height of 5'9" should have a PEF of 450 Litres/Minute.

IV. Aerobic capacity – When we engage in aerobic sports like running or cycling, we are effectively using oxygen to stimulate the heart and lungs to produce energy. When we train in our *aerobic* zone, we are training at a pace that is just below the point where our body will experience excess fatigue, the exact pace of which will vary across individuals. When we train above that level, we enter our *anaerobic* zone where we run the risk of excess fatigue, a situation that we should try to avoid – more on this in Chapter 4.

Aerobic tests are often carried out on a gym-style bicycle using a heart rate monitor so that your fitness instructor can monitor your pulse. You will then be asked to pedal at a set number of reps per minute. Your heart-rate will then be measured at regular intervals whilst you pedal at varying levels of resistance – the more resistance that you can cope with at the predefined number of pedal reps, then the fitter you are. The ultimate aim of the test is to gauge your heart-rate at the point where you experience excess fatigue, i.e. the pace at which you cannot train any harder.

The result of a VO2 Max test is a measure of your maximum oxygen uptake and is expressed in ml/kg/min (i.e. maximum **V**olume **O**xygen). A high VO2 Max figure indicates a high *stroke volume* of the heart. This is the total volume of blood that the heart is capable of pumping in a single beat. Higher training volume will result in a higher blood quantity and means more blood is available to fill the heart. That means that every time the heart beats, the maximum volume of blood is pumped out to the muscles. In Chapter 4 we will look at a number of training practices aimed at improving our VO2 Max.

The VO2 Max values in the tables on the next page (Table 1.2 for men, Table 1.3 for women) will give you some kind of indication as to where you are on the age adjusted scales. For example, if you are a male aged 30-34 and your VO2 Max was calculated as 36 ml/kg/min, then your aerobic capacity is considered as *Average* (Table 1.2). If you are a female aged 35-39 and your VO2 Max was calculated as 46 ml/kg/min, then your aerobic capacity is *Good* (Table 1.3). If your VO2 Max is either *Poor* or *Very Poor*, then it is probably wise to seek further advice from your GP about your suitability to aerobic sports like running.

MEN						
Age	Very Poor	Poor	Fair	Average	Good	Very Good	Excellent
20-24	< 27	27-31	32-36	37-41	42-46	47-51	> 51
25-29	< 26	26-30	31-35	36-40	41-44	45-49	> 49
30-34	< 25	25-29	30-33	34-37	38-42	43-46	> 46
35-39	< 24	24-27	28-31	32-35	36-40	41-44	> 44
40-44	< 22	22-25	26-29	30-33	34-37	38-41	> 41
45-49	< 21	21-23	24-27	28-31	32-35	36-38	> 38
50-54	< 19	19-22	23-25	26-29	30-32	33-36	> 36
55-59	< 18	18-20	21-23	24-27	28-30	31-33	> 33
60-65	< 16	16-18	19-21	22-24	25-27	28-30	> 30

Table 1.2: VO2 Max values for men[3]

WOMEN						
Age	Very Poor	Poor	Fair	Average	Good	Very Good	Excellent
20-24	< 32	32-37	38-43	44-50	51-56	57-62	> 62
25-29	< 31	31-35	36-42	43-48	49-53	54-59	> 59
30-34	< 29	29-34	35-40	41-45	46-51	52-56	> 56
35-39	< 28	28-32	33-38	39-43	44-48	49-54	> 54
40-44	< 26	26-31	32-35	36-41	42-46	47-51	> 51
45-49	< 25	25-29	30-34	35-39	40-43	44-48	> 48
50-54	< 24	24-27	28-32	33-36	37-41	42-46	> 46
55-59	< 22	22-26	27-30	31-34	35-39	40-43	> 43
60-65	< 21	21-24	25-28	29-32	33-36	37-40	> 40

Table 1.3: VO2 Max values for women[3]

AEROBIC EXERCISE AND WEIGHT LOSS

There is no doubt that regular running will help burn body fat, and that *shaping up* is one of the reasons why people take to their shoes. But are aerobic exercises like running an easy solution for addressing weight loss? Consider the following:

> A runner of an average body weight who runs for 60 minutes at an *easy* pace will probably burn around 800 calories. However, there is no guarantee that *all* of the 800 calories will be burnt through fat metabolism as some calories will be burnt from carbohydrates. But given that 1 pound of body fat equates to around 3,500 calories, basic maths tells us that aerobic exercise like running does not burn significant quantities of body fat.

The above example highlights one of the reasons why people can become disappointed with their training endeavours if they go running for the purposes of shedding body weight, albeit with positive intentions. Unfortunately, there are a number of somewhat misleading lobbies of different guises overly promoting the supposed *weight-loss* benefits of sports like running. What happens is that people go out running and increase their distance and intensity without fuelling their body correctly and then end up feeling tired, fatigued and injured. Worst of all, they only lose a very small portion of their body weight that they then gain back after giving up running. So what is the answer?

Firstly, we need to be clear as to why we go running and what we hope to gain from our efforts. In the chapter overview section at the beginning of the book, we briefly looked at some of the main benefits of running, ranging from a healthy heart and lungs and a general feel-good factor, plus of course weight-loss. Fast-forwarding to Chapter 4 and beyond, we will be looking at what the running world is made up of in terms of training practice, cross training, core fitness and running competitions (should you wish to go that far). Then there are the social aspects of running, such as running clubs and training camps. Like most sports, the running community is not short of people and characters. On that basis, running has plenty of fun and fulfilment to offer over and above just weight loss.

Secondly, many of us often observe with undeniable envy some of the faster and perhaps slimmer runners that we see out and about. One of the main reasons why they carry comparatively less body weight is because they integrate their training endeavours with their diet. Clearly, successful running training is about how we train *and* what we eat. When we understand the general dynamics around how the body metabolises fat and carbohydrate, we can then realise the weight loss benefits of being a runner. We can condition our body to burn fat as a source of energy through the development of our *mitochondria*, the part of our muscles where aerobic energy is produced. The more often we go running, then the greater *number* and *size* of mitochondria fibres are created in our muscles. More mitochondria means that we can produce more aerobic energy, which in turn means that we can run faster and for longer. When we run, fats and carbohydrates are transported into our mitochondria where in the presence of oxygen, aerobic energy is then produced. By reducing our carbohydrate intake, we can condition our body to switch to burning fat as a main source of aerobic energy. The more often that we run, then the more we develop our mitochondria capacity, and, coupled with a reduced carbohydrate intake, the more fat will be metabolised, the end result being weight loss. Clearly then, diets that are high in carbohydrates will *inhibit* fat metabolism, whereas diets that are low in carbohydrates will *promote* fat metabolism.

Carbohydrate consumption becomes an important part of our regular diet when we start to train for longer distances or at higher intensities. This is because carbohydrates are the most efficient source of energy for runners. It takes much less energy to burn carbohydrates than what it does to burn fat. However, runners who train at low to moderate intensities do not necessarily need large amounts of *fast* energy derived from carbohydrates. They can get ample supplies of energy from slower burning fat metabolism. In Chapter 3, we will consider *three* different categories of carbohydrate intake that reflect different types of running practice. So carbohydrates are by no means a bad thing. They just have their place in the world of running training practice.

As a general rule, we must never lose more than 1-2 pounds of body fat in any single week. If we were to try and lose more than this amount, the body may switch to using muscle tissue as a source of energy – a situation that will reduce our capacity to store energy. As a result, our everyday strength levels are likely to suffer. We can avoid this situation by losing weight in small and sustainable increments.

Finally, and going back to what we said earlier in the section, it is quite possible that the reason why people don't lose weight as a result of their running endeavours is because they continue to eat carbohydrates and therefore don't give their body an adequate enough chance to switch to metabolising fat. Interestingly, some research from the Karolinska Institute in Sweden back in the 1980s, showed that fat metabolism was 100% higher in *well trained* men when compared to their *untrained* male participants. This just goes to show that fat metabolism through running takes time to develop and will only come as a result of an investment in what we eat *and* how we train our body.

Next steps?

Running Fitness From 5K to Full Marathon caters for beginners as well as experienced runners. You now have a choice as to where you go next. Chapter 2 is aimed at readers who are new to running. Experienced runners may consider looking at Chapter 2 as there are a number of useful warm-up and cool-down routines that might be of interest. Otherwise they can go straight into Chapters 3 and onwards.

References

1 Digate Muth, N. (2009)
   What are the guidelines for percentage of body fat loss?
   American Council on Exercise (ACE). Ask the Expert Blog.
   December 2, 2009
   http://www.acefitness.org/acefit/healthy-living-article/
   60/112/what-are-the-guidelines-for-percentage-of/

2 *Predictive Normal Values for Peak Flow (2004)*
   Nomogram, EU/EN 13826 scale
   http://www.peakflow.com/top_nav/normal_values/index.
   html

3 Stone, J. (2011)
   VO2 Max estimate using Uth – Sørensen – Overgaard – Pedersen
   http://www.johnstonefitness.com/2011/02/14/
   cardiovascular-fitness-hrrest-hrmax-hrr-recovery-hr-and-vo2-
   max/

Chapter 2

Getting Started in Running

Successful running capability is developed in stages, the starting point of which is governed by our current fitness level. This chapter encourages people to develop an initial running stamina in three stages: *Power-walking* and *Jogging*, followed by *Easy-paced* running. By the end of this chapter you will be able to run non-stop for at least 40 minutes to an hour at an *Easy* pace, i.e. a pace that is slightly faster than conversational.

You have the choice as to which stage that you wish to start from depending on how fit you are. During the early stages of running training it is important to develop stamina in a way that is consistent, gentle and sustainable. Try not to set too many deadlines at this stage of your training. You should aim to train 3-4 days a week, but no more than that. The body will adapt much quicker if your training is both regular and consistent. Limit your weekly carbohydrate intake to 20% of your total diet. You should for now get ample supplies of energy from proteins and fats. The training practices in this chapter shouldn't require large amounts of fast energy in the form of carbohydrates.

Invest in comfortable shoes

Wearing a good pair of running shoes is an essential part of being a runner both for comfort and injury prevention. There are shoes designed for casual runners, distance runners, track and field and cross country all with varying levels of comfort and impact protection. It is important to get the right *size* and the right *shape* as this will help prevent unnecessary blisters and foot pain.

Specific shoe sizes and shapes can vary across different brands. When you try on a new pair of running shoes for the first time they should feel comfortable from the moment you stand up in them. Many experienced runners tend to buy their running shoes from people who are runners themselves. Most reputable running specialists employ experienced runners to work on their shop floor for precisely this reason. They are well worth seeking out.

Do your feet pronate at all?

Foot *pronation* is to do with the profile of how the base of the foot impacts with the ground. It is useful to know if you pronate because that will govern what type of shoe to buy. Foot pronation can be monitored either through individual *gait analysis*, or by examining the wear pattern on the soles of an existing pair of well-worn shoes. If there is more wear on the *outer* edges of the sole then it is possible that you *under-pronate* and will require a *Neutral* shoe with plenty of cushioning. If there is more wear on the *inside* of the soles then it is likely that you *over-pronate* and will require a shoe with maximum *support* and *cushioning*. If the wear on the soles is fairly even on both sides then we call this *neutral*. Your local running specialist retailer will be able to help here.

Wear clothes that are comfortable and visible

Running clothing is an industry with no shortage of consumer choice. The various types of shorts, leggings, tops, vests, singlets, thermal wear and summer wear that are available in the shops and on-line all boil down to individual tastes and preferences. Whatever you choose, the following advice is useful:

- Your running clothes should always fit you comfortably. This will help avoid blisters and chafing.

- Use lightweight and breathable clothing that pulls moisture away from your body and dries quickly. This will allow for a more effective regulation of body heat when out running.

- Try and avoid over-dressing during the colder winter months. This is quite a deceptive scenario because once you have warmed-up you will then run the risk of overheating. It might be worth learning to bear the cold a little during the early stages of a run before the body warms up. These kinds of things are learnt through practice.

- Wear clothes that enable you to *be seen* by other road users.

Run safely

When you are out training, always run on the pavements wherever possible. If you need to run on the road then choose the lane that faces any oncoming traffic. For those who go out running when it is dark, always run in well-lit areas. The use of headphones when out running is a potential distraction and is therefore discouraged.

PRE & POST-TRAINING ROUTINES

Warming-up before training and then cooling-down afterwards is an important part of getting the most out of training, keeping injuries at bay and preparing for the next training session. This section introduces a number of simple warm-up and cool-down drills that are well known to the running community. By the end of the next couple of sections you will be able to start formulating a few of your own drills.

Example pre-training warm-up drills

The purpose of a warm-up drill is to increase the heart rate and body temperature and loosen up some of the key muscle groups. During a warm-up, blood circulates more rapidly around the body vitalising the main aerobic organs like the heart and lungs.

Warming-up before exercise is synonymous with driving a motor vehicle from a cold start. The fuel consumption and engine wear are going to be comparatively higher up until the engine has achieved a normal running temperature, where from that point onwards the fuel consumption will optimise. Warming-up before running training follows a similar kind of analogy and aims to avoid the following problem scenarios:

- Injury, i.e. pulling a muscle that has not yet *woken up*.

- Feelings of premature fatigue, i.e. being tired too soon.

This section details *six* example basic stretches that runners are encouraged to do before training. Before starting the warm-up routine below, it is good practice to do a **gentle 3-5 minute walk or jog**, whichever suits you best. Once you have done this, your first exercise is **Sideways leg swings**.

1. Sideways leg swings

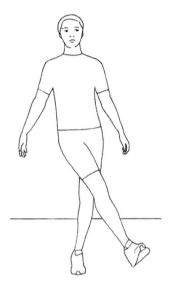

Purpose: To loosen up the hips and engage the glutes.

Technique: Stand upright and gently swing your leg across your body using your arms to maintain a balance. Keep your leg straight when doing so and ensure that your pelvis faces forward.

Repetitions: Complete *two* sets of 10 swings each to the left and to the right.

2. Forward leg swings

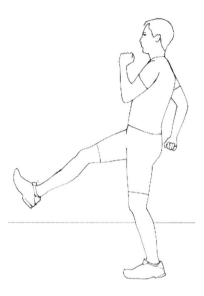

Purpose: To loosen up the hips and engage the quadriceps, hamstrings and glutes.

Technique: Stand upright and gently swing your leg forwards and backwards away from your body using your arms to maintain a balance.

Repetitions: Complete *two* sets of 10 swings each to the left and to the right.

3. Walking lunges

Purpose: To loosen up and engage the hip flexors and quadriceps.

Technique: Stand upright and then step back with one foot. Squat down until your lower leg is parallel to the floor. Try not to step *too* far back. Keep your upper body upright. Engage your stomach and abdominals and use your arms to maintain a balance. Hold for about a second and then alternate.

Repetitions: Complete *two* sets of 10 lunges each to the left and to the right.

4. Butt kicks

Purpose: To loosen up and engage the quadriceps, hamstrings and glutes.

Technique: Stand upright and raise one knee so that your quadriceps muscle is nearly parallel to the ground. Whilst keeping your knee high, kick the back of your heel upwards and towards your buttock area. Alternate on each side, using your arms to generate a rhythm.

Repetitions: Complete 10 alternating kicks.

5. Body hugs

Purpose: This is the first of two stretches aimed at loosening up the shoulders. This is an ideal stretch for people who spend large amounts of time driving a car or at a desk in front of a computer screen. Having relaxed shoulders is an important part of developing an efficient running technique.

Technique: Stand upright and place your hands over the opposite shoulder. Gently push down with your hands and pull the elbows towards the top of your stomach. Hold for 30 seconds before gently releasing. Rest for 5 seconds.

Repetitions: Complete the stretch 3 times.

6. Arm back

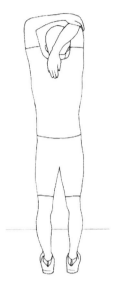

Purpose: This is the second of the two shoulder exercises and is practiced for similar reasons to the previous exercise *Body hugs*.

Technique: Stand upright and place your hands behind your shoulder. Place your opposite hand on the elbow and gently push your arm backwards. Hold for 30 seconds before gently releasing. Rest for 5 seconds and then swap sides.

Repetitions: Complete the stretch 3 times on each side.

Example post-training cool-down routine

After you have completed a training session of about 30 minutes or more, it is important to recover in time for the next training session. When we stop after a training session, our heart rate will drop and our muscles will start to contract. A cool-down routine marks the start of the *next* training session, hence the importance of a cool-down routine. Generally speaking, there are three things that we need to watch out for during the first 60 minutes *after* we have finished training:

> I. **Pulling a muscle** – When we stop training, problems like pulling a muscle can occur when we don't manage the cool-down process through appropriate stretching.

> II. **Hunger and dehydration** – We should aim to eat and drink something within 1-hour as this is when the body will absorb food intake more efficiently. Water is by far the most effective means of rehydration, and foods based on protein and carbohydrates are good for recovery.

> III. **Catching a chill** – When our body cools down after training, we must allow our body temperature to return to normal at a uniform rate. Adding an extra layer of clothing within 5-10 minutes of finishing training (sooner in colder conditions) is generally what most runners tend to do after training.

The remainder of this section details *four* basic example cool-down stretches that are well known to the running community. When applying a stretch, use your own body weight and stretch until a mild pain is felt. Be aware that *over-stretching* can cause injury.

Your first cool-down stretch is **Quadriceps** (next page).

1. Quadriceps

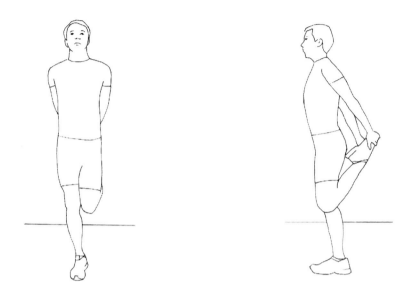

Purpose: To lengthen and strengthen the quadriceps. This is an important cool-down stretch because every time you either lift your foot off the ground when running or touch the ground with the foot, the quadriceps are engaged.

Technique: Stand upright and maintain a forward facing position. Grab your foot from behind and pull the heel upwards towards your buttock. Pull on the toes and push your chest gently outwards keeping your knees together. Hold for 30 seconds before gently releasing. Rest for 5 seconds and then swap sides.

Repetitions: Complete the stretch 3 times on each side.

Variation: This stretch can be modified by using *both* hands to pull the heel towards the buttock (as per the *right-hand* picture above).

2. Hamstrings

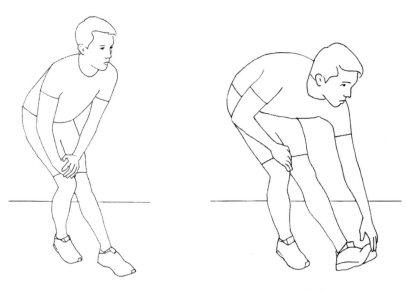

Main hamstring stretch   **Variation**

Purpose: To lengthen and strengthen the hamstrings. This is an important cool-down stretch because like the quadriceps, every time you either lift your foot off the ground when running or touch the ground with the foot, the hamstrings are engaged.

Technique: From a standing position, take a short step forward with one foot. Lean forward and place both of your hands on the forward knee. Squat down on the forward side and gently straighten your forward leg. Hold for 30 seconds before gently releasing. Rest for 5 seconds and then swap sides.

Repetitions: Complete the stretch 3 times on each side.

Variation: This stretch can be extended further by reaching down to the forward foot and pulling back your toes engaging your calf muscles (as per the picture to the right of the main hamstring stretch).

3. Upper calf (Gastrocnemius)

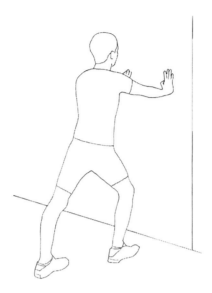

Purpose: This is the first of two calf muscle stretches aimed at lengthening and strengthening the lower leg muscles. These are important cool-down stretches because every time your foot touches the ground when running, the calf muscles and Achilles heel are engaged.

Technique: Stand with both hands against the wall and with the feet a hip's distance apart. Step forward with one foot and straighten the rear foot. Push both your pelvis and the forward knee towards the wall to engage your upper calf muscle. Hold for 30 seconds before gently releasing. Rest for 5 seconds and then swap sides.

Repetitions: Complete the stretch 3 times on each side.

4. Lower calf (Soleus)

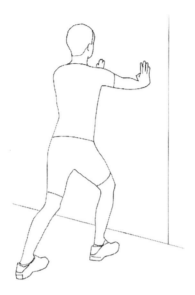

Purpose: As per the *Upper calf* muscle stretch.

Technique: Stand with both hands against the wall and with the feet a hip's distance apart. Step forward with one foot and drop the knee of your rear leg very slightly. Push both your pelvis and the forward knee towards the wall to engage the lower calf muscle. Hold for 30 seconds before gently releasing. Rest for 5 seconds and then swap sides.

Repetitions: Complete the stretch 3 times on each side.

THREE STAGES OF INITIAL RUNNING DEVELOPMENT

Getting into a regular running routine is not difficult. Three stages of running development are presented in the sections that follow. Those new to running may like to start from Stage 1 with a power-walking regime before developing into jogging at Stage 2. Experienced sports players, or perhaps those who are returning to running after a break from the sport, may prefer to go in at Stage 2 and start off with some jogging intervals and then develop from there.

What pace should I be aiming for at for each of the 3 stages?

Our pace when we do exercise is governed by our heart-rate. Training pace is normally expressed as a percentage of our Maximum Heart Rate (MHR). Our MHR is the *maximum* number of beats that our heart is capable of ever doing in one minute.

The simplest method of gauging our individual MHR is to use the *age* related formula of *220 – Age*. For example, someone 35 years old will have a MHR of about 185 Beats/Minute (220 – 35). If they were to run at a pace of 75% MHR then their heart-rate will be around 139 Beats/Minute (75% x 185), or thereabouts. We would obviously need to wear a heart-rate monitor to know this for sure.

MHR is a very useful way of expressing how fast or how slow different types of training need to be to ensure that our training is of a *quality* nature. The use of a heart-rate monitor for the purposes of this chapter is useful, but not essential. For now, the age-related formula should be sufficient.

Throughout this book we will be using *six* different training paces all of which are summarised in the Glossary: *Power-walking, Jogging, Easy, Steady, Threshold* and *VO2 Max*. Power-walking, Jogging and Easy-paced running are the focus of this chapter and are summarised as follows:

Stage 1: Power-walking is fast and brisk walking at about 125% of your normal walking speed. If your average walking speed is 3mph, then your power-walking speed is going to be just under 4mph.

Stage 2: Jogging is running at a pace that is *conversational*, i.e. you should be able to talk to someone running next to you. If you are using a heart-rate monitor then your jogging pace is about 60-65% of your MHR.

Stage 3: Easy-paced running is running at a pace slightly faster than your jogging pace, and is about 65-70% of your MHR.

Stage 1: Power-walking

Newcomers to running should power-walk regularly for about 45 minutes every other day for about 8 weeks. This is a great way of conditioning the key muscle areas that are mobilised when running. Once you have developed a level of fitness that you are happy with then have a think about moving to Stage 2 and introduce some jogging intervals into your sessions.

> The advice I have for beginners is the same philosophy that I have for runners of all levels of experience and ability — consistency, a sane approach, moderation and making your running an enjoyable, rather than a dreaded part of your life –
> *Bill Rodgers, winner of four Boston and four NYC marathons*

Stage 2: Jogging

Jogging (or intervals of jogging) forms the basis for developing further into running. Firstly, we need to take a look at how we develop a good jogging technique as basis for becoming a runner.

Developing an efficient jogging technique

The development of an efficient jogging technique is an important and ongoing part of regular training. The following three sub-sections consider some of the basic ideas around how to develop a good running technique:

I. Foot strike – When we are running, we must try and hit the ground with the ball of the foot first. We must then lower the heel towards the ground before going back up onto the ball of the foot and then pushing ourselves away with the toes. Running like this helps us avoid running on our heels and is therefore a good way of reducing the impact on our knee and hip joints.

II. Forward movement – When we are running, most of our body movement is in the forward direction. We should aim to keep both our hips and shoulders *level* when running with no unnecessary sideways movement or twisting. This is a highly effective way of developing *forward propulsion*.

III. A relaxed and upright posture – We should try and keep our shoulders relaxed with our arms high and our elbows bent. Our elbows should not go past the front of our body as this causes unnecessary body twisting.

The three areas outlined above help us become more conscious of what we are actually doing when we run. You are encouraged to practice the three basic ideas outlined above in your jogging and running intervals in Stages 2 and 3.

Example power-walking and jogging interval combinations
A good way of introducing jogging into the equation is to start with equal intervals of power-walking and jogging. As you become fitter and better at jogging, you can eliminate power-walking altogether. The goal of this training stage is for you to be able to jog non-stop for 40 minutes before moving to Stage 3.

To start off with, you could do *two* sets of 10 minutes of power-walking followed by 10 minutes of jogging, a total training time of around 40 minutes. The aim of the exercise is to reduce the power-walking intervals whilst increasing the jogging intervals. You could do this in 2-minute increments, i.e. 8-minute power-walk with a 12-minute jog for each set, then 6-minute and 14 minutes, and so on. You need to decide for yourself what works best. Further guidelines around how to get the best from the training schedule are as follows:

- Always warm-up at the beginning of a session, and cool-down at the end.

- Aim to train every other day.

- As a general guideline, increases in jogging time intervals should be no more than 10-20% in any week.

- As you progress through this stage, find a power-walking and jogging combination that you are comfortable with and then make further power-walking reductions when you are ready to do so (this is down to you as the individual).

- If you find a particular combination too strenuous, then increase the power-walking time for the next 2 weeks and progress from there.

Move on to Stage 3 once you can complete a non-stop 40-minute jog.

Stage 3: Easy-paced running

Introducing easy-paced running is done in a similar way to how jogging intervals were included in Stage 2. The goal of this stage is to be able to run non-stop at an easy pace for at least 40 minutes to 1-hour. To start off with, and in a similar way to what we did in Stage 2, you could do up to *three* sets of 15 minutes jogging followed by 5 minutes of easy-paced running. Then it is just a case of *reducing* the jogging element by 2 minutes and *increasing* the running element by the same amount and then seeing how get on. Once you can run for at least 40 minutes to 1-hour non-stop, then you are well on your way towards practising some of the higher intensity training techniques outlined in Chapter 4. You can also congratulate yourself on becoming a runner!

Further training in advance of Chapter 4

As we move into Chapter 3, our focus shifts to Nutrition and Hydration, an interesting and important part of playing sport. We will then return to running training in Chapter 4 and explore the core training practices that are aimed at developing endurance and performance. In the meantime, there are a few small amendments that you could make to your hourly training sessions that will put you in a good position for what we will be covering in Chapter 4:

I. Speed intervals – Include a 1-minute speed interval in every 10 minutes of running. This will start to condition your *fast-twitch* muscles for speed training. You should try and run *fast* but *not* flat-out as you may get injured. We must develop our speed performance in incremental stages and will be discussed more fully at various points throughout Chapter 4.

II. Shallow hills – Depending on where you live, try and include in your training route a few short hills and undulations (you may have already had no choice!). This will start to strengthen your hamstring, quadriceps and calf muscles for further hill training in Chapter 4.

Chapter 3

Nutrition and Hydration

Eating the right foods will have a direct and noticeable effect on your general success and performance in running. The goal of this chapter is to communicate nutrition and hydration in a way that is scientifically correct, easy to understand and results in better quality running experiences and performances. This chapter is split into three parts as follows: *Food Diet*, *Training Nutrition* and *Fluid Intake and Hydration*.

PART I: FOOD DIET

When we understand the basic scientific effects that food types can have on the human body when consumed, we can draw the correct conclusions about the foods that runners should eat and in what quantities, and perhaps those they should avoid. Foods that contain Protein, Fats and Carbohydrate form the bulk of what we eat on a daily basis.

Protein – Foods like meat, fish, eggs and nuts are great sources of protein and everyday energy and are foods that we have been eating since the beginning of time. Foods that contain proteins contain many of the important vitamins and minerals needed for everyday life. Protein also plays an important role in a post-run recovery by helping to repair and re-build damaged muscle fibres. Proteins also contain *leptin*, a hormone that helps to suppress our appetite and boost our everyday metabolism. Runners are encouraged to include sufficient amounts of proteins in their daily food diets.

Fats – The consumption and inclusion of fat in our diets is a well known and ongoing source of discussion; the primary reason being the confusion around foods that *contain* fat, and foods that *cause* fat cells to be created in the body. An explanation is as follows:

I. Saturated fats are commonly found in foods like meat and eggs along with *unprocessed* natural dairy products like full-fat yoghurt. Despite the bad publicity about the consumption of saturated fat, there is no evidence to suggest that these kinds of foods cause life threatening illnesses, such as heart disease and other cardiovascular problems, when consumed as part of a healthy balanced diet[1: p105-111]. Foods that contain *monounsaturated* fats, such as nuts, avocado, olives and olive oil, are also not considered to be harmful as are *omega-3 polyunsaturated* fats normally found in fish. The presence of these kinds of fats in our diet is an important source of energy for runners. Like proteins, saturated fats also contain *leptin*. Runners are also encouraged to include sufficient amounts of fats in their daily food diets.

II. Industrially produced fats (or *partially-hydrogenated* and many *trans-fats*) are examples of foods that have been modified in ways that go against the body's *self-regulatory* systems, i.e. our ability to metabolise foods *efficiently*. Foods like biscuits, crisps, cakes, pastries, fruit juices with added sugar – to name but a few – are all foods that run the risk of causing the body to generate body fat particularly when we consume them in excess. Some of these foods are also known as *simple carbohydrates* (discussed below) and are best avoided.

Carbohydrates – Carbohydrates provide our body with the glycogen that it needs to function properly during exercise. When we consume carbohydrates, they are rapidly converted into glucose. As glucose levels in our blood start to increase, the pancreas produces *insulin*, a hormone that takes glucose from the bloodstream and converts it into glycogen which is then stored in our muscles and liver for future use. *Glycogen* is a critical source of energy particularly for performance and endurance runners – more on this later. There are two types of carbohydrates that runners need to be aware of:

I. Complex carbohydrates such as brown-rice, wholemeal bread, white potatoes, whole-grain pasta, porridge, muesli and granola take time to break down into glycogen (energy derived from carbohydrates). These kinds of *good* carbohydrates are stored in our muscles and liver. They provide us with fast and efficient sources of fuel in the form of glycogen during running training.

II. Simple carbohydrates, such as foods with added sugar, starches and dairy products like margarine, are absorbed into our bloodstream much quicker than complex carbohydrates. These kinds of foods are known to cause surges in insulin and subsequent blood sugar levels that only last for a short period of time (30-60 minutes) before sharply dropping back again. Spikes in blood-sugar levels will also cause short-term peaks and troughs in energy levels. Dehydration is also another potential problem because water is needed to absorb glucose. These kinds of *bad* carbohydrates add very little value to a runner's daily diet and are best avoided.

Proteins, fats and carbohydrates – What are the differences?

The main differences between proteins, fats and carbohydrates focus around *insulin*, a hormone that is responsible for storing fat in the body. If we consume carbohydrates but don't burn off glycogen through exercise (energy derived from carbohydrates) then it will get converted into body fat. As a result, excess carbohydrate consumption will cause the body to create fat cells, a situation that will ultimately lead to weight gain. This is one of the general reasons why we need to be careful around our carbohydrate consumption, irrespective of how much running we do.

The body processes proteins and fats very differently. Proteins also produce insulin but also produce *glucagon*, a hormone that mitigates the fat-creating effects of insulin by stimulating the *breakdown* of fat cells; a process that helps to maintain stable blood glucose levels. Fats however don't produce any insulin response and therefore don't promote the creation of fat cells in the body. This is why, generally speaking, we should stock up on plentiful amounts of proteins and fats.

Carbohydrate requirements and subsequent metabolism is related to training quantity. When we run, our body will burn varying proportions of fat and carbohydrate with small amounts of protein, the absolute proportions will depend on training *distance*, *pace* (or *intensity*) and body conditioning. Carbohydrates provide more energy per unit of oxygen compared to fat. We cannot run as fast on energy from fat metabolism as we could on carbohydrates.

The body would struggle to breakdown fat cells quickly enough to create an ample supply of energy to service the needs of the aerobic organs like the heart and lungs. Runners who train for performance and endurance will require varying quantities of carbohydrates in their diets. This will provide fast and efficient sources of quick energy that are ideal for developing speed and distance.

Carbohydrates are also important for the purposes of preventing *glycogen depletion*, an adverse situation that arises when we inadvertently allow our glycogen stocks to drop too low. The consequence of glycogen depletion is a sharp drop in running speed, and in extreme cases, a complete stop.

How much carbohydrate?
Total carbohydrate intake for the purposes of running training is based on duration and intensity. The following three categories provide some useful guidelines around carbohydrate consumption:

CATEGORY I: Up to 60 minutes of easy-paced training – As we have already seen, carbohydrates are the most efficient source of energy for the purposes of developing speed and distance. But everyday runners who train continuously for about an hour at an *easy* pace of around 65-70% MHR don't necessarily require a high demand for fast energy derived from carbohydrates. Runners in this category could easily condition their body to metabolise fat as a good source of energy whilst metabolising comparatively smaller amounts of carbohydrate.

Supplies of fat are generally not a problem for most runners as the human body stores fat very efficiently. Someone who weighs 80Kg (176 lb) with a body fat percentage of 15% has 12Kg (26.5 lb) of their body weight made up of fat. Given that 1Kg (2.2 lb) of fat provides about 7,500 calories of energy, this equates to about 90,000 calories worth of energy stored in the body as fat. Clearly, a healthy supply of fat as a source of energy is not an issue for most runners.

Carbohydrate consumption for this particular category is around 2-4g (1-2g/lb) of carbohydrate per Kg of body weight for a runner who trains for about 60 minutes a day at an easy pace. Someone who weighs 80Kg will require around 160g to 320g per day of carbohydrate (80Kgx2g=160g and 80Kgx4g=320g). Given

that 1g of carbohydrate supplies around 4 calories, their carbohydrate intake would be between 640 and 1,280 calories per day for
running activities. They would also need to stock up on adequate
supplies of proteins and fats.

CATEGORY II: Up to 60 minutes of higher-intensity training –
Runners in this category may like to consider increasing their
carbohydrate intake to provide faster and more efficient energy
for the purposes of high intensity training like *VO2 Max* and
Threshold (Chapter 4).

As a general guideline, an average runner who trains continuously for about 60 minutes a day that includes varying levels of
speed type training will require around 5-7g of carbohydrate per
Kg of body weight (2.5-3g/lb). Someone who weighs 80Kg
will require around 400g to 560g per day of carbohydrate
(80Kgx5g=400g and 80Kgx7g=560g). Given that 1g of carbohydrate
supplies around 4 calories, their carbohydrate intake would be
between 1,600 and 2,240 calories per day for running activities.
They would also need to stock up on adequate supplies of proteins
and fats.

**CATEGORY III: 60-90+ minutes training for performance and
endurance** – The use of carbohydrates as a fast and efficient source
of energy for the purposes of training for performance and
endurance is a practice of which dates back as far as the 1960s.
There is no denying that runners from many walks of life have
successfully achieved a variety of running related sporting
achievements as a result of including carbohydrates in their diets.

When we train continuously for longer than 60-90 minutes, our
body will start to burn fat more efficiently. This is because a higher
volume of training will increase the quantity and size of *mitochondria*,
the part of our muscles where aerobic energy is produced. When
we train regularly and consistently for extended periods of time,
our fat metabolism will increase. In the process of doing so, our
body will also preserve carbohydrate stocks – more on that later.

Absolute carbohydrate consumption can vary across this
category of runner. The *slower endurance runner* who trains for
longer than 60-90 minutes at a pace of anything *up to* 75% MHR

could probably survive on a carbohydrate intake similar to that of a *Category II* discussed earlier (5-7g per Kg of body weight), and still avoid glycogen depletion. However, a *faster endurance runner*, like (e.g.) someone who is perhaps intending on running a fast full marathon at 75-80% MHR, would require a higher quantity of carbohydrates. Faster runners from this category who train continuously for 2-3 hours would aim to consume around 8-10g per Kg of body weight to prevent glycogen depletion. Therefore, someone who weighs 80Kg would need a carbohydrate intake of between 2,560 and 3,200 calories per day for running activities (80x8x4 calories=2,560 and 80x10x4calories=3,200). They would also need to stock up on adequate supplies of proteins and fats. Furthermore, although research has found that efficient fat metabolism gives an advantage to distance runners, the advantage actually disappeared when the training intensity was increased. In other words, some runners experienced glycogen depletion when they tried to run a *fast* long distance race on a carbohydrate intake similar to a *Category II* outlined earlier. But faster distance runners found that to mitigate the risk of glycogen-depletion, an increased carbohydrate intake was needed as a way of fuelling their body more efficiently when running at a higher heart rate. Fat metabolism by itself simply wasn't enough. This is why the higher *Category III* carbohydrate intake is recommended for faster distance runners.

To prevent glycogen depletion as a result of running faster and for longer, we must also condition our body to preserve carbohydrates (this was briefly mentioned earlier). One way of doing this is to purposely run low on glycogen stocks towards the end of a training session. This will send a signal to our body that it needs to preserve carbohydrates in the future. As we continue practising our long runs, our body will know that it needs to preserve glycogen stocks, and continue to use fat metabolism as a key source of energy. This kind of conditioning will take time to develop.

The consumption of carbohydrates should be spread throughout the week. If you are planning on doing a long run on a Sunday morning, then you should plan to increase your carbohydrate consumption from around Thursday or Friday. This is to ensure that you have adequate stores of glycogen in advance of a long run scheduled for the weekend.

Despite the guidelines around carbohydrate consumption for this particular category, not all runners are able to consume the recommended quantities of carbohydrates. One reason could be that their body is simply not used to that particular type of food and as a result may struggle to digest the required quantity. This means that many endurance runners must train their body to be able to digest the recommended quantity of carbohydrates, and like many other aspects of training, this will take time to develop. In the meantime, and while the body adapts to consuming and storing carbohydrates efficiently, glycogen depletion is likely to be a potential problem during longer runs, a situation that can be addressed through the use of energy supplements *during* training as way of topping-up glycogen stocks. Many runners struggle in the latter stages of longer distance races either because they don't understand their carbohydrate requirements, or because they haven't practiced glycogen replenishment. Energy replenishment is a very important part of distance training and is discussed in Part II later in the chapter.

What kinds of foods should athletes eat?

The discussion around nutrition generally concluded that we can eat protein and fats in plentiful amounts, but we need to be a little careful where carbohydrates are concerned. We should try and avoid simple carbohydrates and processed foods.

What foods can I eat in plentiful amounts?	
Meat	Beef, pork, chicken, lamb. This includes the fat on the meat and the skin on the chicken
Fish	Fatty fish like salmon, herring and mackerel. Shellfish. Tuna in moderate quantities
Eggs	All types (e.g.) boiled, poached, fried (with Olive Oil), omelettes
Fats	Butter and full-fat cream. olive oil and coconut oil
Vegetables	Cauliflower, cabbage, asparagus, brussels sprouts, onions, spinach and mushrooms. These are grown *above ground*
Salad	Lettuce, cucumber, celery, radish and tomatoes
Dairy products	Full-fat yoghurt, sour cream, cottage cheese, goat's milk
Fruit	Mainly berries and avocado
Nuts	All types

What foods can I eat in moderation? These are foods that can be consumed occasionally.	
Alcohol	Red wine is known to be good for the digestion system. Spirits are fine but stay away from sugary mixers
Tea and Coffee	These are great short-term stimulants provided that they are not consumed in excess. Decaffeinated variations are a much better alternative
Fruit	Citrus fruits apples, oranges and grapefruits contain *natural sugar* but have many nutrients that are considered good for everyday health
Dark Chocolate	Contains 70% cocoa and with that goes a comparatively lower sugar content

What foods should I avoid? These are either manufactured or processed foods (or bad carbohydrates) and are difficult to digest or have a high-sugar content.	
Sugar	Biscuits, drinks with added sugar or artificial sweeteners.
Fat	Crisps, pastries, starches, sunflower oil
Dairy products	Yoghurt with added sugar, margarine

Performance and endurance runners who include varying proportions of carbohydrates should always eat *good* carbohydrates like brown-rice, wholemeal bread, white potatoes and whole-grain pasta.

Example meal plans and ideas for runners

The foods that we eat at various points throughout the day will have an effect on how we perform during our training sessions. This section considers some simple ideas around what to eat for breakfast, lunch and evening meal as well as what snacks to eat during the daytime. Many runners limit their intake of refined foods and other food preservatives by making up their own meals using fresh and natural produce. This is all a matter of individual choice.

Breakfast provides vital sources of energy to start the day and is the most important meal of the day if you are a runner. If you are doing fair amounts of long distance and high intensity training, starting the day on an empty stomach is not recommended. Indeed, some runners go running before breakfast to help kick-start their metabolism early, a process that helps to burn body fat. People who skip breakfast create the risk of feeling hungry later in the day, and then spend the rest of the day picking at foods that don't suppress their appetite. The following foods are ideal for breakfast as they contain varying amounts of easily digestible proteins and carbohydrates that are ideal for stocking up on energy reserves:

- Cereals like muesli, granola or porridge.
- Toast or bagel with jam, marmalade or honey.
- Pancakes or waffles with syrup.
- Scrambled or poached eggs.
- Full fat yoghurt with added fresh fruit (optional).
- Fruit smoothies
- On the morning of a race, an energy drink or an energy bar

Lunch is an ideal way of maintaining your energy reserves during the day particularly if you are training in the evenings. It is important to eat well during the daytime especially if you lead a busy lifestyle. There is nothing worse than starting a training session on an empty stomach only then to risk the possibility of glycogen depletion halfway through. The following lunch plans are designed to help maintain everyday energy levels and provide varying quantities of carbohydrates that are required for training:

- Omelettes cooked with olive oil (with added vegetables).
- Meat or fish sandwiches or wraps with added salad.
- Fresh salad with eggs or fish and optional potatoes.
- Soup.
- Fresh fruit.

An **evening meal** is normally considered the main meal of the day and is an opportunity to replenish our core energy reserves for the next day. An evening meal designed for a runner is one that is rich in proteins and varying quantities of carbohydrates, the latter of which is based on training level (pages 42–45). The example meal suggestions below are typically high in proteins, but offer an element of choice around carbohydrate quantity:

- Meat stew with added vegetables.

- Chilli or curry with rice.

- Roast chicken, lamb, beef, pork or turkey with vegetables.

- Spaghetti Bolognese.

- Pizza with side salad.

Snacks offer an effective means of stocking up on energy levels during the day. A runner's appetite can be quite high and so eating snacks are a good way of dealing with bouts of hunger that occur in between meals. The following suggestions around snacks are designed to give a feeling of fullness whilst at the same time provide incremental sources of energy in advance of a training session:

- Rice cakes.

- Cottage cheese.

- Energy bars.

- Granola bars.

- Mini pizzas.

Meal timing issues

The timing of meals during the daytime is an important consideration particularly if you are in a period of focused training. There are two scenarios that are worth taking into account to ensure that you get the balance right between your training quantity and food intake:

I. The timing of your main meal – If you train in the evenings then you may consider having your main meal at lunchtime and opt for a smaller quantity of food in the evenings after finishing a training session. This is a good strategy for two reasons. Firstly, by eating

48

earlier in the day you will ensure that you have an adequate supply of energy in time for training, and secondly, to limit any potential disturbances to your sleeping patterns by going to bed on a full stomach. On the flip side however, it is still better to eat later in the day in advance of doing a longer run the following morning.

II. Eat small amounts frequently – There is a high chance that we will feel hungry more often during periods of regular training. This kind of scenario is particularly common amongst those training for a longer run, like (e.g.) a full marathon where general food metabolism will be comparatively higher than other runners. Nevertheless, to prevent this kind of scenario from becoming a problem, runners should still have their three core meals each day, but consume regular but small snacks in between meals as a way of overcoming short-term hunger.

Food consumption during a training session

When we are training, at least 70% of our energy is being used to generate aerobic energy – we would expect this given the high intensity nature of running. As a result, bodily functions, like the digestive system, are given a lower priority. Runners are therefore encouraged to avoid eating too many solid foods during training as this may result in feelings of bloatedness and stomach cramps. If we do need to stock up on energy supplies during an extended training session (mainly to prevent glycogen-depletion), we are better off using an energy supplement like a gel or an energy drink. These kinds of foods will digest into our system much quicker. Energy supplements are discussed in the next part.

PART II: TRAINING NUTRITION

Most reputable sports retailers will stock a variety of *energy* and *recovery* products in the form of drinks, bars and gels. Many of these products contain electrolytes such as magnesium, sodium and potassium that are essential for carbohydrate metabolism and muscle function. Athletes from various disciplines use these kinds of products for the purposes of their training. The promotion and resulting uptake amongst the athlete running community has been typically quite high. Most runners will test a few products, find the ones that they like and then use them in their training endeavours.

Like most foods, not all products suit everyone. Certain types of *gels* for example contain caffeine, which might not suit everyone.

Replenishment and recovery

Energy supplements are used for three primary purposes: *Pre-loading*, *Replenishment* and *Recovery*:

I. Pre-loading – Many endurance runners will consume an energy bar within an hour of commencing a long run. Energy bars are a great source of carbohydrates and are highly applicable to runners who train for extended periods of time. For non-endurance runners, and in particular those who train for under an hour, energy bars might be a little overkill. It is more than possible to get ample supplies of energy from everyday foods, but this is all a matter of individual choice.

Many runners might have an energy drink prior to starting a training session to increase their blood sugar levels. Bearing in mind that many energy drinks are simple carbohydrates, the good thing is that these kinds of drinks are absorbed into the bloodstream very quickly and are ideal for pre-training purposes. It is generally good practice to take an energy drink with some water as well to help absorb the glucose into the bloodstream.

II. Replenishment – Energy supplements like drinks and gels are useful for replenishing our fluid and glycogen stores during training and will enable us to train for extended periods of time. For a runner who trains beyond the 90-minute time limit, and depending on how much carbohydrate their body can consume and digest in the days prior to training, and how efficient their body is at burning fat reserves as a source of energy, they may need to replenish their glycogen stocks *during* training to prevent glycogen-depletion. The most effective way in which to do this is to carry energy supplements during a training run for consumption as and when required. Some runners (e.g.) can train for anything up to 2 hours without having to take on extra energy reserves. Other runners who are just starting to practice regular longer runs may need to start replenishing from around 60-90 minutes, but this will start to increase to 90-120 minutes and beyond, as their body conditioning makes a shift towards preserving carbohydrates and burning more fat.

III. Recovery – After a training session lasting for more than 30 minutes, it is important to stimulate the body's recovery process by consuming foods that contain a combination of carbohydrates and protein. These kinds of foods are ideal for recovery purposes and should be consumed within an hour of completing a training session. This is the period when the body will absorb food most efficiently and will also help you recover in time for the next training session.

Runners have a choice as to how they go about recovery. They can either make their own foods and bring them along to training sessions, or alternatively, purchase a recovery product from a specialist running retailer.

How best to consume energy supplements

Over-consumption of energy drinks can cause dehydration. This is known to happen when endurance runners stock up their glycogen reserves using sugar-based supplements believing that these products are also useful for the purposes of rehydration, when in fact not all of them are. We need to be careful here and *always read the label*, so to speak. Be sure to take energy drinks with some water if you are in any doubt. There is a difference between glycogen replenishment (to prevent *glycogen-depletion* – already covered) and rehydration (to prevent *dehydration* – more on this in Part III).

The consumption of energy drinks during the daytime in advance of an evening training session is highly discouraged. This type of carb-loading is a dubious practice that will cause short term peaks and troughs in blood-sugar levels lasting anything from 30 minutes to 1-hour. Runners are better off sipping water during the day and consuming the recommended amounts of complex carbohydrates as a way of ensuring adequate carbohydrate supply in advance of a training session.

Energy supplements are not substitutes

Given the marketing around energy products and the potential value that they can bring in our running endeavours, the truth is that these products don't actually make us physically stronger. An energy drink (for example) will help an endurance runner maintain a pre-trained pace for an extended period of time, but this is only within the limits of their overall fitness. Energy products are supplements and must never be considered a substitute for a bad diet or an inadequate training schedule. Either way, we still have to do the leg work.

PART III: FLUID INTAKE AND HYDRATION

Keeping ourselves hydrated is a critical part of any sport training. Our individual water consumption depends on a number of factors ranging from training mileage and intensity, body size and weight, outside temperature and how easily we sweat.

What is sweating?
As a general rule, about 75% of energy that we put into exercise gets converted into heat. That is why our body gets warmer when we train. To keep our body cool and within safe temperature limits, much of this heat is dissipated in the form of *sweat* and is the main reason why body fluid replacement is a critical part of training. On that basis, the general guidelines around fluid intake for runners basically says that if you think you are thirsty then you probably are thirsty and therefore need to take on board some fluids. You will only have a short and finite time to act and this will vary across individuals.

What is dehydration?
When we dehydrate our body runs out of the element that is designed to keep us cool when we exercise; that being water. During dehydration, our blood will thicken and the efficiency of our heart will be reduced. This will cause our heart rate and body temperature to increase and will result in a dramatic reduction in running performance. Dehydration can come on very quickly.

General guidelines for water consumption

Fresh water is by far the best form of fluid to drink either before, during or after training. If you work during the day and do training in the evenings, then it is good practice to regularly sip water. Keeping a bottle of water handy is a good way of getting into the habit of keeping well hydrated during the day. Fluid hydration and rehydration is a process that takes time and should not be hurried. Try and avoid shortcuts by taking on large amounts of water in one go particularly just before a training session.

The most useful indicator of hydration is urine colour. Water should be consumed in regular quantities that ensure our urine is pale yellow in colour. A dark yellow colour suggests low body fluid levels and therefore an increased risk of dehydration. A clearer colour suggests an above average fluid level and the risk of *saturation*.

How much water should I consume before training?
About 60% of our total body weight is made up of water. Generally speaking we should aim to drink about 2 litres of water per day as a baseline requirement. You should look to take about 500ml of water about 1-2 hours before a training session and a further 150ml just before the start of a training session.

How much water do I need to consume during training to prevent dehydration?
The best way of gauging the amount of water that was consumed during a training session is to weigh oneself before a training session and then again at the end of a training session. For example, if you lost 0.5Kg (1.1 lb) of body weight during a 1-hour training session, and given that 0.5Kg of body weight equals about 500ml (17 fl. oz) of water, then you would need to have drunk at least 500ml of water during training. In warmer conditions, we may need to consume anything up to 50% more water.

Post-training rehydration
After training and as part of your recovery, you should aim to consume at least 1.5 times the amount of water that you consumed during training. For example, if you consumed 500ml (17 fl. oz.) of water in a training session then you need to take 750ml (26.5 fl. oz.) of water after training. You could drink 250ml or so within 30 minutes of finishing training and then sip the remaining quantity every 10 minutes or so until your rehydration target of 750ml has been reached. Much of this is down to individual practice.

What do I do if I inadvertently dehydrate?
In the unfortunate event of dehydration, the only viable option is to stop training and walk back to base. Recovery from dehydration is normally achieved through a healthy dose of water, something to eat plus a good night's sleep. Extreme cases of dehydration and exhaustion can result in hospitalisation, but these situations are quite rare.

Over-hydration is counterproductive and potentially dangerous

Given the growing popularity of running and the hysteria that goes with dehydration, many runners incorrectly *over-consume* with water. Many running commentators also believe that running *fatigue* is only caused through dehydration. But this isn't the whole truth given that *glycogen depletion* can also cause fatigue and a drop in running performance.

Over-hydration can give rise to *Hyponatremia*, an adverse medical condition that can cause two things to happen. Firstly, the body rejects the excess fluid. Persistently having to stop and discharge body fluids during training is both inconvenient and unnecessary. Secondly, it reduces the concentration of sodium in the blood, a chemical that helps *digest* and *retain* fluid. The consequences of over-hydration are known to cause situations like nausea and disorientation and in very extreme cases, brain seizure.

The best way of avoiding the side effects of over-hydration is to consume an energy drink that contains sodium, and not consume more water than you would have lost during training.

Tea and coffee
The consumption of caffeinated tea and coffee before or after training should be consumed in moderation. After taking on water at the end of a training session, many athletes will indulge tea or coffee simply because of the short-term stimulating feel that it provides. This is more of a personal thing than an essential training necessity.

Alcohol

During periods of sustained training, alcohol should be consumed in moderation, if at all. There is nothing wrong with occasional alcohol intake, but given the adverse effects that alcohol consumption can have on the nervous systems plus the high level of carbohydrate, training under the effects of the mildest of hangovers is not a great strategy. Many runners tend to avoid alcohol consumption during periods of training particularly in the run up to a competitive race.

References

1   Briffa, J. (2012)
    Escape the diet trap
    Fourth Estate (Harper Collins)
    ISBN: 978-0-000-744243-0

Chapter 4

Training for Performance and Endurance

To be successful in running will require the mastery of several different styles of training practices. Throughout this chapter we will be looking at six types of training practice specific to running: *Recovery, Speed, Hills, Long runs, Race pace* and *Rest*. At the end of the chapter we will be looking at some of the common causes of sporting injuries and how we can overcome them. Firstly though, we will look to further develop our p*re* and *post* training drills by including some extra stretches into our routines.

ADVANCED PRE & POST TRAINING STRETCHES
As a follow-on from the basic pre and post-training stretches described and illustrated in Chapter 2 (pages 24–29, 31–34), this section introduces further stretches that are more applicable to the higher intensity sessions discussed in this chapter. Runners are encouraged to include these stretches in their warm-up and cool-down drills.

Further pre-training stretches
Warming-up before a training session will help prevent injury and premature fatigue. This chapter introduces *five* additional stretches useful for the purposes of warming-up. Try and engage your abdominals and stomach muscles when performing these stretches. This is generally good for core development. Before doing any stretching, do a gentle 3-5 minute jog. Once you have done this, your first exercise is **High knees**.

1. High knees

Purpose: To stretch and loosen up your quadriceps. Can be performed either on the spot or over a short distance.

Technique: Stand upright and raise one knee so that your quadriceps muscle is parallel to the ground. Quickly alternate with your other leg using your arms to generate a rhythm.

Repetitions: Complete 10 reps.

2. High arms and knees

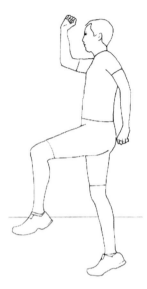

Purpose: To stretch and loosen up your quadriceps. Can be performed either on the spot or over a short distance.

Technique: Stand upright and raise one knee so that your quadriceps muscle is parallel to the ground. Raise your opposite elbow. Then spring up from your standing foot and jump upwards from the toes. Alternate on each side and repeat the sequence in a hop and jump rhythm.

Repetitions: Complete 10 reps.

3. Calf raise

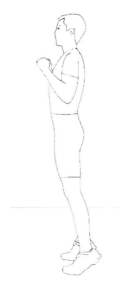

Purpose: To stretch your Achilles heel and lower calf muscles.

Technique: Stand upright and push upwards on your toes. Hold for a second and then return your heels to the floor.

Repetitions: Complete 3 raises.

4. Trunk rotators

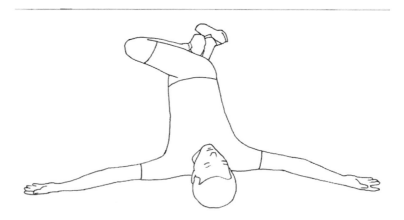

Purpose: To stretch your glutes and buttock muscles.

Technique: Lie down on the floor and spread your arms out. Cross one leg over the other leg and place your foot on the other side of the opposite knee. Roll your pelvis over and look upwards. Hold for 30 seconds and then change sides.

Repetitions: Complete 3 rotations on the left and the right sides.

5. Trunk side

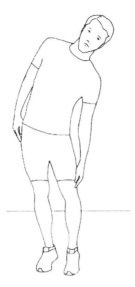

Purpose: To stretch the muscles on the side of the trunk.

Technique: Stand upright and keep your hands by the side. Gently lean the body to one side and slide the hand down the side of the leg. Do not lean forwards or backwards or allow your knees to bend. Hold for 30 seconds and then change sides.

Repetitions: Complete the stretch 3 times to the left and to the right.

Further post-training stretches

This chapter presents *eight* further example stretches that can be included in a cool-down routine. As always, when applying a stretch, use your own body weight and stretch until a mild pain is felt. Be aware that *over-stretching* can cause injury.

The practice of higher intensity and longer distance training may require us to make changes to the timing of our cool-down routine. If we are feeling tired and fatigued after a training session then we should do a *delayed* recovery to avoid stretching fatigued muscles. A delayed cool-down is when we don't stretch immediately after training but instead go home, bath or shower and eat something within the hour (as recommended), and then later when we are feeling more relaxed, we can do a quick 3-5 minute warm-up of (e.g.) running on the spot before completing our usual cool-down stretching routine. This is a much better way of cooling down after a hard training session.

Your first cool-down stretch is **Glutes and lower back** (next page).

1. Glutes and lower back

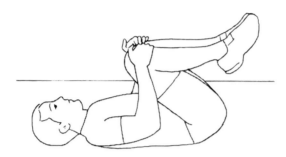

Purpose: To stretch the glutes and lower back muscles.

Technique: Lie down on the floor and raise both of your knees off the ground. Place your hands on the knees and pull them towards your chest. Keep your knees close together and the back of your head flat on the ground. Hold for 30 seconds and then change sides.

Repetitions: Complete the stretch 3 times on each side with a 5-second break in between each one.

2. Hamstrings (leg straight using a resistance band)

Purpose: To stretch the hamstring muscles. Can be performed using a towel as an alternative to a resistance band.

Technique: Lie down on the floor. Place the resistance band around the back of your foot under the arch. Clutch each end of the band with your hand. Raise your leg and push your foot upwards into the air. The aim of the exercise is to keep your leg straight and at right angles to the floor. Keep the opposite leg slightly bent and the back of your head flat on the floor. Hold for 30 seconds and then change sides.

Repetitions: Complete the stretch 3 times on each side with a 5-second break in between each one.

3. Hamstrings (bent knee using a resistance band)

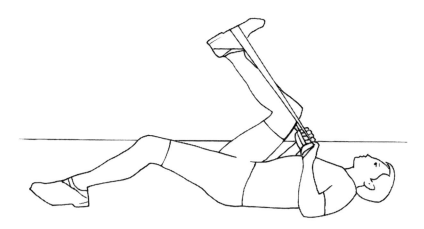

Purpose: To stretch the hamstring muscles. Can be performed using a towel as an alternative to a resistance band.

Technique: Lie down on the floor. Place the resistance band around the back of your foot under the arch. Clutch each end of the band with your hand. Raise your leg and bend at the knee. Using the band, pull the knee towards your stomach, whilst pushing your foot up into the air. Keep the opposite leg slightly bent and the back of your head flat on the floor. Hold for 30 seconds and then change sides.

Repetitions: Complete the stretch 3 times on each side with a 5-second break in between each one.

4. Upper back

Purpose: To stretch the upper back and shoulders.

Technique: Stand upright and put both of your arms out in front and join your hands together at the fingers. Push forwards with both shoulders and straighten the arms. Keep looking straight ahead. Hold for 30 seconds before gently releasing.

Repetitions: Complete the stretch 3 times with a 5-second break in between each one.

5. Hip flexors

Purpose: To stretch the hip flexors and quadriceps.

Technique: Stand upright and step back with one foot nearly as far as the leg will reach. Squat down slightly until your knee is just off the ground keeping your body upright. Use your arms to maintain balance and posture and keep looking straight ahead. Hold for 30 seconds before gently releasing.

Repetitions: Complete the stretch 3 times on each side with a 5-second break in between each one.

6. Adductors

Purpose: To stretch the adductor inner thigh muscles.

Technique: Sit down on the floor and bring your feet together. Place your hands around your ankles and place each elbow to the side of the knee. Then lean forward slightly and gently push your elbows onto the knees whilst keeping hold of the ankles. Keep looking straight ahead. Hold for 30 seconds before gently releasing.

Repetitions: Complete the stretch 3 times with a 5-second break in between each one.

7. Glutes

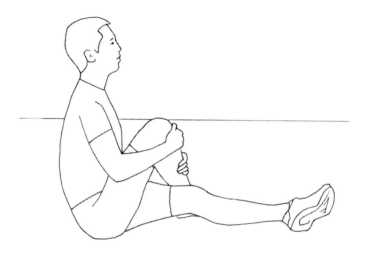

Purpose: To stretch the glutes and abductor muscles.

Technique: Sit down on the floor with an upright posture and with your legs straight. Bring one foot over the other leg. Place your hands around the knee then gently pull the knee towards the body. Try and sit upright and look straight ahead – it is important not to slouch. Hold for 30 seconds before gently releasing.

Repetitions: Complete the stretch 3 times on each side with a 5-second break in between each one.

8. Piriformis

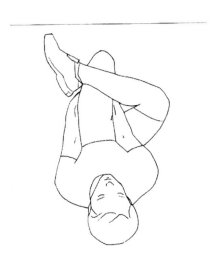

Purpose: To stretch the piriformis, hamstring and glute muscles.

Technique: Lie down on the floor with both of your knees bent. Raise one knee close to the chest. Bring your other foot over the raised knee and position the ankle just above the knee. Grab the raised leg with your hands and then pull your knee close to your chest. Keep your head flat on the ground. Hold for 30 seconds before gently releasing.

Repetitions: Complete the stretch 3 times on each side with a 5-second break in between each one.

TRAINING FOR PERFORMANCE AND ENDURANCE

In running training, it is those who include a healthy balance of performance and endurance training with appropriate amounts of rest and recovery tend to be those who persistently perform well in running. Clearly, the more we train in a certain way (or *ways*) then the more efficient our body will become at performing those particular activities. For example, the more speed training we do then the faster we will be able to run. The more often we practice long runs then the further we will be able to run. The more we practice a particular target race pace, the greater chance we have of achieving a PB in a competition. Finally, and just as importantly, the more we practice rest and recovery, then the more time we allow our body to adapt to a higher level of ability, and not to mention, keep injuries at bay. These are some of the example reasons why consistency and regularity in training are such important aspects of our training irrespective of what we are aiming for.

Training in warmer conditions

Successful and effective training in warmer conditions is about conditioning our body to function in hotter temperatures to prevent situations like dehydration and heat exhaustion from happening. The following useful tips should reduce any possibility of heat-related problems:

I. Adapt your pace – You will need to adjust your running pace and condition your body to cope with a warmer climate. The more often that you train in warmer conditions, then the more your body will adapt and the easier you will find warm weather training.

II. Reduce the intensity of your warm-up – A gentle warm-up would be sufficient in most cases. It will not take the body that long to start gently perspiring.

III. Start hydrating earlier – As we learnt back in Chapter 3 (pages 52–55), the body can use anything up to 50% more fluid in warmer conditions. To prevent dehydration, start taking on water sooner than you would normally do.

IV. Watch your sodium levels – Sodium is found in most reputable energy drinks and helps to maintain the body's fluid balance. Energy products are very good for warm-weather training but must be taken with water to prevent dehydration (especially products with high sugar content). *Hyponatremia* is another adverse medical condition associated with a significant drop in sodium levels caused through *over-hydration* (previously covered in Chapter 3 page 54).

Training in colder conditions

As well as training in warmer conditions and climates, there are a number of things that we need to be aware of when we train during the winter months:

I. Extra clothing – Many runners may choose to wear a *dri-fit* type base layer and add at least one extra layer of clothing to cope with lower temperatures and wind chill. The body may take a little longer to get warm during the winter but most runners will just grin and bear the cold at first. On the flip side, avoid getting *too* warm by over-dressing as this can cause dehydration and other heat related issues.

II. Adjust your recovery time – Some runners may reduce their recovery times during training sessions like *Threshold*, *VO2 Max* and *Hills* (discussed later). This all depends on how quickly your body temperature drops during a recovery period. If you find yourself getting cold during a recovery period, then you might like to reduce (e.g.) a *3-minute* recovery by 30 seconds to just two and a half minutes.

III. Hydration requirements don't change by very much – Water intake and rehydration during the cold must not be scrimped on. Water consumption in the winter months might be less than what it might be during the summer, but it is not by very much.

Increases in training quantity – How much?

Over-training should be avoided to help prevent injury and illness. As a general guideline, increases in training *distance* or *intensity* should be limited to about 10% in any week. Exact increases are likely to be governed by fitness levels and will therefore vary across individuals.

Useful points to note before starting

The example training sessions for *VO2 Max, Threshold* and *Hills* that are outlined later in the chapter are categorised into three levels. You will need to decide which level to start from depending on your general fitness level and running experience. The three levels are summarised as follows:

Level 1 training is for those who have been training for 10-15 miles a week for at least 6 months and have had very little exposure to high intensity training like speed and hills. They may have also started running as a result of following Chapter 2.

Level 2 training is for those who have been running 20-25 miles a week for at least 2 years and may have taken part in a few half marathon races (13.1 miles) and achieved a time of at least 2 hours. This person may also indulge in other sports like cycling, swimming and core fitness.

Level 3 training is for those who have been running for at least 3 years and may have successfully achieved a half marathon time of at least a sub 1:45. They may also indulge other sports and be confidently aspiring to run a sub 4-hour full marathon.

For the purposes of simplicity, each of the schedules has an *even* number of intervals. This means that when you go out and train, you can take an *out and back* approach, i.e. starting from a fixed base (e.g., a road junction or a lamppost), eight intervals would be out and back *four* times.

Sections 1 through to 6 below consider *six* different training practices that promote an all-round approach to running. The first of the six training practices that we will be considering is **Recovery**.

TRAINING PRACTICE #1: RECOVERY

The practice of *recovery* applies to several of the training practices discussed in this chapter. Recovery is about helping the body to return to normal after training and help stimulate improvements in our fitness. Our individual ability to recover from running training is governed by a number of factors, including age, lifestyle, diet, sleeping patterns, fitness level and training history. Recovery in running training is practiced in three ways:

I. Short-term recovery happens when we stop training for a fixed period of time *during* a training session to allow our heart-rate to temporarily recover in time for the next training interval. During a recovery period of (e.g.) 3 minutes, you may stretch a little, sip some water or gently jog around to stay warm.

An inadequate recovery period means that we don't give ourselves enough time to get our breath back. On the other hand, when we give ourselves a too longer recovery period, we allow our body to cool down by too much making it more difficult to get going again. Both scenarios will have the potential to reduce the quality of training.

Aerobic recovery test

How quickly we recover from a training session is a useful measure of fitness and is easily done by checking your pulse before and after you have completed a run. The test goes like this:

- Before setting out for a run, count your pulse for 30 seconds. Double the value to give you a number in beats per minute (e.g., 70 beats/minute). This is going to be a value that is *close* to your resting pulse rate.

- After completing a run of at least 40 minutes at a steady pace, stop running and immediately count your pulse for 30 seconds. Double that number to give you roughly what your pulse would have been for a minute.

- Check your pulse again 30 seconds later and then repeat this process *two* more times.

After 3-4 minutes of completing your run, you should have 4 pulse values that indicate your heart-rate in beats per minute. The rate at which your pulse drops back down to a value close to your resting pulse rate is a gauge of how well you recover after doing aerobic exercise. If you did this test every week for about 8 weeks then you will be able to monitor changes in your aerobic development.

II. Post-training cool-down routines are made up of two elements:

A. Stretching after a training session is an important part of remaining injury free. Runners should by now have developed their own stretching routines and be using them regularly in their training practice.

B. As already highlighted in Chapter 3 (pages 39 and 51), we should stock-up on some protein and carbohydrates after a training session to aid the recovery process. Runners are encouraged to do this within *1-hour* of completing a training session. Food consumption beyond that time limit will significantly reduce our body's ability to absorb glycogen and is sometimes the reason why we perhaps might feel tired the day after training. Protein is good for repairing damaged muscle tissue and carbohydrate consumption is an important part of glycogen replenishment. It can take anywhere between 24-48 hours to fully replenish our glycogen stocks during periods of sustained training.

III. Recovery runs are slow and gentle jogs that are normally done within 24 hours after a harder training session like a long run. The aim of a recovery run is to loosen the muscles, improve blood supply to the legs and help our body to adapt and improve as a result of much harder training sessions. Many successful runners include recovery sessions in their training endeavours because they realise the importance of not overwhelming their body in ways that limit the ongoing development of their physical or aerobic fitness.

Generally speaking, your recovery runs should be run at a pace of between 65-70% MHR (or *Easy*-paced running). Anything faster is likely to be *too* fast and potentially counterproductive. This is why it is important to distinguish between a *regular* training session and a *recovery run* – many runners do their recovery runs too hard and then fail to recover properly in time for their next training session. This is another example of *over-training* and is best avoided.

TRAINING PRACTICE #2: SPEED TRAINING

VO2 Max and *Threshold* training are two well known types of running practice that are considered in this section. There are four main reasons why we practice speed training:

I. Enhanced Peak Expiratory Flow (PEF) – When we run at speed, our heart rate will sharply increase. This means that we have to breathe in a large quantity of air into our lungs to provide enough oxygen to deliver a certain quantity of aerobic output through the muscles. Speed training sessions are designed to enhance PEF.

II. Increased heart-stroke volume – Speed practice develops the *stroke volume* of the heart. The stronger our heart then the more blood will get pumped into our muscles. As a result, our *VO2 Max* will improve.

III. Develop the Type II fast-twitch muscle fibres – Speed training will condition our Type II *fast-twitch* muscles. These particular muscle fibres are capable of producing large amounts of muscle force very quickly. The more often that we practice speed the more fast-twitch muscles will be developed. As a result, we will run faster.

IV. Mental preparation – For those who are looking to compete, running at a fast pace will require focus and strength of mind. Practicing speed is therefore a great way of developing internal stamina.

Threshold training (or *tempo* as it is often referred) is when we run at 80-90% MHR and is about developing speed over a sustained distance. This kind of speed training is popular with runners training for distances of 10K-10 miles, or more. *VO2 Max* training is when we run at a pace above 90% MHR but is comparatively faster running but in shorter bursts. VO2 Max training is popular with runners training for distances like 5K and 10K.

The speed sessions that are presented in this particular section are *interval* based where you will be given varying amounts of recovery time in between each speed interval. Many runners refer to this type of training as *fartlek* (or *speed play*), i.e. alternating intervals of running fast and then slow. VO2 Max and Threshold training are discussed in the two sub-sections that follow along with some example training plans. Firstly, let us take a look at VO2 Max training.

VO2 MAX TRAINING
VO2 Max (or *Maximum Oxygen Uptake*) is a body weight adjusted measure of the maximum rate at which our body is capable of consuming and processing oxygen when running (measured in

ml/kg/min). Our VO2 will be at its maximum when we *run* (and therefore *breathe*) as hard as we can. One simple way of practicing VO2 Max is to run flat out for about 6 minutes. Any period longer than that is going to be unsustainable simply because you will reach exhaustion point (i.e. you will *max* out).

VO2 Max training schedules

The Level 1 VO2 Max training focuses on 60-second intervals before progressing up to 90-second intervals. Levels 2 and 3 focus on 3 and 5-minute intervals, respectively. Beginners or runners with no previous experience of high-intensity training are advised to start at *Level 1* and develop their speed and stamina gently. Experienced runners have the choice as to which level that they wish to start from. Before each VO2 Max session, complete a 5-10 minute jog and then complete your usual pre-training warm-up routine. VO2 Max sessions can be quite tough and so be sure to stretch and strengthen your quadriceps, glutes, calf and hamstring muscles. At the end of the session, recover by stretching, rehydrating and eating within an hour.

The training schedules below have been presented as *timed* intervals. If you have access to a 400 metre track then you can convert the times into respective distances, i.e. 200m, 400m, 800m, etc. This is all a matter of choice.

Level 1 VO2 Max training

Level 1 introduces some simple shorts bursts of 60-second intervals with a 60-second recovery (or *60/60* intervals). This is to help you gauge how fast you *can* actually run. As you find 60/60 intervals a little easier, you can develop further into slightly longer 90/90 intervals.

Level 1 *Stage 1* VO2 Max training summary (60/60 intervals):

- Run as fast as you can for 60 seconds and then walk for 60 seconds.
- Build up your speed gently and maintain a consistent pace.
- Complete the 60/60 seconds combination 12 times.
- Practice this session for 4-6 weeks and see how you get on.

Consider moving to Stage 2 and practicing 90/90 intervals once you have developed a fast and consist pace throughout the 60/60 intervals in Stage 1.

Level 1 *Stage 2* VO2 Max training summary (90/90 intervals):

- Run as fast as you can for 90 seconds and then walk for 90 seconds.
- Complete the 90/90 seconds combination 10 times.
- Maintain a very fast and consistent pace.

Level 2 VO2 Max training

Level 2 VO2 Max training uses 3-minute intervals with a 2-minute recovery. You should run as fast as you can throughout the 3-minute interval and maintain a consistent but very fast pace. Take advantage of the recovery period by doing a gentle jog.

Level 2 VO2 Max training summary:

- Run for 3 minutes and then gently jog for 2 minutes.
- Complete the 3/2 minute combination 6 times.

Level 3 VO2 Max training

Level 3 VO2 Max training uses 5-minute intervals with a 3-minute recovery. As in Level 2, you should run as fast as you can throughout the 5-minute interval and maintain a consistent but very fast pace. Gently jog during the 3-minute recovery.

Level 3 VO2 Max training summary:

- Run for 5 minutes and then gently jog for 3 minutes.
- Complete the 5/3 minute combination 3 times.

Optional: Gauging your MHR using VO2 Max training

Back in Chapter 2 (page 35) we used an age-related formula for gauging our Maximum Heart Rate (MHR). Now that you have completed some VO2 Max training and know what it feels like to run fast, you can use these experiences to better gauge your MHR.

The test below is best done after a few days rest from running. This is so that you can perform at your highest intensity. You will also need to use a heart rate monitor. Here is the test:

- Warm-up thoroughly by doing a 10-15 minute jog followed by your usual stretches.

- Then, run as hard as you can for 3 minutes.

- Check your heart rate every 10 seconds during the interval and remember the *largest* value (Note: the largest value is not necessarily going to be your heart rate at the point you stop after 3 minutes – it is possible for heart rate to peak at any time during the interval).

- Stop and recover for 3 minutes.

- Complete the 3-minute interval three more times each with a 3-minute recovery noting your largest heart rate value.

- Cool-down thoroughly by completing a 5-minute jog followed by your usual stretches.

Your MHR is going to be the largest value that you recorded throughout the three intervals.

THRESHOLD TRAINING

Training at threshold level is when we run at a pace of about 80-90% MHR. For most runners, this is either the speed at which we could race at for about 50-60 minutes, or 2-3 word pace, i.e. you should be able to say no more than 2-3 words before being out of breath. The regular practice of threshold training dates back as far as the 1980s and is popular with distance runners. Your precise MHR at threshold will depend on your own level of individual aerobic fitness. Less experienced runners will threshold at the lower end of the scale (i.e. closer to 80% MHR), whereas a faster and more experienced runner will threshold at the upper end (i.e. closer to 90% MHR). Threshold training sessions should last for no more than an hour depending on individual fitness level and experience.

Threshold training schedules

Threshold training is best developed in stages. Beginners, or runners with no previous experience of high-intensity training, are advised to start at *Level 1* and endeavour to run *as close to* their threshold as is possible. Experienced runners can look at either Levels 2 or 3 and will be expected to either train at *just on* their threshold pace, or *just over*.

Before each threshold session, complete a 5-10 minute jog and then complete your usual pre-training warm-up routine. Threshold sessions can also be quite tough and so be sure to stretch and strengthen your quadriceps, glutes, calf and hamstring muscles. Be careful not to burn out too early in a threshold session. Prior to setting out, you will need to find an uninterrupted stretch of road. You should aim to do half of the session in one direction, and the second half as the return leg from where you started from (See *out and back* approach – page 73). At the end of the session, recover by stretching, rehydrating and eating within an hour.

Level 1 threshold training

Level 1 threshold training introduces the basic ideas around speed endurance and provides an opportunity to gauge your threshold pace.

Level 1 Threshold training summary:

- Complete 4 x 6-minute threshold intervals.

- Run at 2-3 word pace, or thereabouts.

- Take a 3-minute recovery between each interval. Walk for the first 30-60 seconds then jog for the remaining 2 minutes.

- Total training time: 33 minutes (excluding warm-up and cool-down).

If Level 1 was too difficult and you perhaps only completed 3 out of the 4 intervals, then try reducing the threshold interval from 6 minutes down to 5 minutes. Alternatively, increase your recovery period from 3 minutes to 4 minutes. We must avoid slowing down and reducing the pace during threshold training as this will defeat the object of the exercise. If on the other hand you found Level 1 too easy then there are a number of options to consider:

- Reduce the 3-minute recovery period by 30 seconds..

- Increase the threshold interval from 6 minutes to 7.

- Progress to *Level 2* and see how you get on.

Level 2 threshold training

Level 2 threshold training is about developing a consistent 2-3 word pace. You should aim to run at *just on* your threshold pace throughout each interval. Running any faster may result in muscle fatigue, one of the likely causes being excess *lactate* in the blood.

Lactate is a bi-product of carbohydrate metabolism that is created during aerobic exercise. When we train in our *aerobic* zone (i.e. *just on* our threshold pace), our body produces and consumes lactate in similar quantities. When we train above and beyond our aerobic zone into our *anaerobic* zone, we are expecting our body to process energy at a rate that is unsustainable, the result being *excess* lactate: a situation that will prevent our muscles from contracting efficiently and one that will cause a drop in running performance. Level 2 threshold training aims to mitigate the possibility of excess lactate problem by encouraging us to train at *just on* our threshold pace.

Level 2 Threshold training summary:

- Complete 4 x 8-minute threshold intervals.

- Run at a consistent 2-3 word pace – this should be *just on* your threshold pace.

- Take a 3-minute recovery between each interval – walk for the first minute and then jog for the last 2 minutes.

- Total training time: 41 minutes (excluding warm-up and cool-down).

Level 3 threshold training

Level 3 threshold training takes speed training one step further where we are running at a pace that is *just above* our threshold pace.

This is when our body starts to generate excess lactate in the bloodstream, a situation that is likely to cause excess muscle fatigue. Regular threshold training however, enables us to condition our body to use excess lactate as a source of fuel. This is where excess lactate is distributed away from the harder working muscles such as the legs and is used instead to provide fuel to other areas of the body like the heart, the brain and the liver – the result is a better all-round running performance. This is a process known as *lactate shuttling* and was identified by George Brooks from the University of California, Berkeley, USA. This kind of threshold training where the body is able to process and quickly recover from elevated lactate levels is a more advanced way of training aimed at more experienced runners.

Level 3 Threshold training summary:

- Complete 4 x 10-minute threshold intervals.

- Aim to run at a pace that is about *3-5 seconds per mile quicker* than your threshold pace.

- Take a 2-minute recovery jog between each interval.

- Total training time: 46 minutes (excluding warm-up and cool-down).

Optional: Gauging your heart-rate at threshold

If you are interested in knowing your exact heart-rate when running at threshold, then any reputable sports clinic or laboratory will have the facilities to measure this. Gauging our heart-rate at threshold is done by taking small blood samples at various heart-rates whilst you run on a treadmill. Your heart-rate at threshold is just below the point at which your blood lactate production exceeds consumption.

TRAINING PRACTICE #3: HILL TRAINING

Hill training (or hill reps) is practiced for two primary reasons. Firstly, to develop the required strength in the calf, hamstring and quadriceps muscles that are critical for hilly courses; and secondly, to develop speed performance on the flat. A large part of being successful in hill training is achieved through the development of uphill and downhill technique, both of which are described as follows:

I. Uphill running technique:

- Running uphill requires shorter strides than you would normally do on the flat. The steeper the hill, the greater the number of strides. As a result, your calf, hamstring and quadriceps muscles during hill training will work quite hard.

- Develop an efficient running technique by relaxing your shoulders, keeping your elbows high and your arms moving backwards and forwards using them to generate power.

- Maintain an upright posture by looking towards the crest of the hill, and not at your feet.

II. Downhill running technique:

- Lengthen your stride as you accelerate down the hill. The steeper the gradient, the greater the stride length.

- Aim to land on the balls of your feet with your legs bent to reduce knee impact.

- Maintain a slightly wider and rotating arm position to maintain balance.

- Try and float down the hill with light footsteps. Try not to *brake* when running downhill as this can cause excess fatigue in the legs.

- Be sure to use the downhill descent to recover in time for the next uphill climb.

Hill training schedules

Level 1 hill training uses short hills done at a steady pace and are aimed at those with little or no previous experience of hill training. Level 2 and Level 3 hill training use longer hill distances and are geared towards more experienced runners. As with all training, it is important to develop technique and stamina in a way that is sustainable. Be careful not to burn out too early in a hill session.

The location of hill training is largely dependent on where you live. For this reason the schedules only specify an indicative hill distance. Ideally, you will need a hill with a gradient of between 1:3 to 1:15, and with a distance ranging from about 75 to 350 metres. As an option, there are several commercially available mapping products that enable you to measure running routes and more accurately gauge hill profiles.

Before each hill session, complete a 5-10 minute jog and then complete your usual pre-training warm-up routine. Hill sessions can be quite tough and so be sure to stretch and strengthen your quadriceps, glutes, calf and hamstring muscles. At the end of the session, recover by stretching, rehydrating and eating within an hour.

Level 1: Short hill reps at a steady pace

Hill training at Level 1 is fairly straightforward. We simply run at a steady pace to the top of the hill, and gently walk or jog back down to the bottom.

Level 1 Hill reps training summary:

- Approximate hill length: 75 metres (150m up and back).
- Complete 6 hill reps for a single set increasing to at least 10 reps as you progress over time.
- Aim to complete at least **three** sets with a 3-minute recovery between each set.
- Run up the hill at a pace no higher than 80% MHR.
- Recover by walking or jogging back down to the bottom of the hill.

If you found the Level 1 hill session too difficult then perhaps reduce the number of hill reps. You can then resume back up to 6 reps at a later date – bear in mind that 10 reps is the target and so there is plenty to aim for here. If you found that the 3-minute recovery was inadequate, then perhaps increase your recovery to 3.5 minutes or possibly 4 minutes – try not to recover for longer than 4 minutes.

Level 2: Medium hill reps at 5K pace

Hill reps at Level 2 are much harder because we are attempting to run at your 5K pace but with the added resistance of a gradient.

Level 2 Hill reps training summary:

- Approximate hill length: 200 metres (400m up and back).
- Complete 4 hill reps for a single set.
- Aim to complete at least **three** sets with a 3-minute recovery between each set.
- Run up the hill at your 5K pace.
- Recover by running at a steady pace back down to the bottom of the hill.

Level 3: Longer hill reps at an even speed

Hill reps at Level 3 are all about completing both the uphill and downhill parts in the same amount of time. This kind of hill training is geared more towards experienced runners. The exact pace for each hill rep will vary across individuals. You may want to start off by running each rep at your 10K pace and develop a faster rep time as you progress.

Level 3 Hill reps training summary:

- Approximate hill length: 350+ metres (at least 700m up and back).
- Complete 3 hill reps for a single set.
- Aim to complete at least **three** sets with a 2-minute recovery between each set.
- Choose a fast pace that you are comfortable with and focus on being able to run up and down the hill in the same amount of time.

Further hill training

Success in hill training comes from being able to run up and down longer and steeper hills in quicker times and at higher paces.

Runners who are interested in developing further in hill training may like to consider the following variations in training:

I. Cross country – Many runners take part in cross country races during the winter seasons to develop their strength and speed in advance of any road races scheduled for the spring season. These kinds of events are also popular with road runners given the reduced impact that goes with off-road training. Many road runners find that it just makes a change to do something different.

I. Threshold – Many runners include an element of hill training in their threshold runs, the practicality of which will depend on where you live. Using a blend of threshold, hills and long runs (next section) is good training if you are looking at doing races that are hilly and undulating.

TRAINING PRACTICE #4: LONG RUNS

Long runs (continuous running for 1-hour or more) are an important part of developing strength and endurance for distances of about 10 miles and upwards. Weekly mileage increases should be limited to around 10%, or thereabouts. Ideally you should find a distance that you are comfortable with and stick with it before making any further increases. Long runs are an important part of endurance training for the following reasons:

I. Improve VO2 Max – When we improve our VO2 Max, we enhance the stroke volume of the heart, i.e. the total quantity of blood that the heart is capable of pumping to the muscles in one single beat. As we develop our mileage, our heart and lungs will become more efficient at processing oxygen for longer periods of time, a critical part of running endurance. If we increased our weekly training mileage too sharply, then we run the risk of excess muscle fatigue, a situation that often arises as a result of *over-training*. We should reduce our training to a more manageable level, and go from there.

II. Build endurance and base mileage for distance training – Long runs develop the Type I *slow-twitch* muscle fibres. These muscles take longer to fatigue and are therefore more efficient at using oxygen for extended periods of time. If we are training for a (e.g.) 1:45 half marathon time and we didn't do at least 60 to 90 minutes of continuous running training on a weekly basis, then we would lack the baseline aerobic conditioning required for endurance running. To run distance, we must develop base miles, and it is often those who struggle in the latter stages of a race do so because of a lack of base mileage development.

III. Fat metabolism – The development of our mitochondria muscle fibres will increase at a faster as a result of doing long runs. A larger quantity of bigger mitochondria will enhance our overall aerobic output capability, and in the process of doing so, will promote an increased level of fat metabolism (Chapter 1 page 18, Chapter 3 page 43).

IV. Mental preparation – Running for extended periods of time requires an element of psychological strength. Mental preparation is a critical part of being able to run longer distances, and long runs are a great way of preparing oneself for this kind of challenge. It is only through the regular practice of long runs will long runs become easier.

Success in long run training is normally measured in two ways: either by how quickly you can run a certain distance relative to how quickly you ran it on a previous attempt, or if you compete, your race performances. If your race times are coming down, then base mileage training coupled with any speed training is a having a positive effect.

Long run training strategies

Successful beneficiaries of long runs (e.g., full marathon runners) develop their endurance capability in two ways. Firstly, they practice their long runs at a pace 10-15% slower than their target race pace. For example, a runner with a target race pace of 8-minute miles who is planning a 90-minute long run would start out with a pace of 9:22-minute mile and increase that to around 8:48-minute/mile during the latter stages of the training run. Practicing long runs like this during the early stages of base mileage development helps to prevent over-training by leaving enough energy for harder speed sessions during the week.

The second way of developing endurance capability is by running a portion of a long run at a target *race pace*. For example, a runner with a target race pace of 9-minute miles who is planning a 90-minute long run would start out with a pace of about 10-minute/ mile and then complete the final 30 minutes of the run at the target race pace of 9-minute/mile. The advantage with including race pace intervals in long runs is that we give ourselves the chance to practice our race pace so that we know what that pace actually feels like. A *long slow run* will probably result in a *long slow race* if we didn't include race pace training.

Avoid glycogen-depletion and dehydration

Back in Chapter 3 we learnt that nutrition forms a critical part of long run training. As a general rule of thumb, when we train for more than 60-90 minutes and depending on how efficiently we have trained our body to store ample supplies of glycogen in our muscles and liver, we may need to stock up on glycogen levels and rehydrate. Using some of the metrics in Chapter 3 (Carbohydrate intake pages 42–45, Replenishment and Recovery pages 50–51, Hydration pages 52–54), you can calculate the following quantities as part of your long run planning and before setting out:

- How much carbohydrate will you need to consume in the 2-3 days before the long run?

- How much of that carbohydrate quantity will your body be able to consume and digest (remember that you may need to condition your body over a period of time to store glycogen)?

- How much carbohydrate in the form of energy supplements will you need to carry with you to prevent glycogen-depletion?

- How much water will you consume during the run?

- How much water will you need to carry with you to prevent dehydration?

Once you have understood your training pace relative to your expected race pace plus your glycogen and hydration cycles, then you will be well on the way to achieving success in long distance running.

Many runners wear a waist-band during their long runs that include a water carrier and a pouch for carrying (for example) energy gels. Your local running specialist should be able to help here.

TRAINING PRACTICE #5: RACE PACE

The development of race pace is a critical part of being successful in competitions. One of the main reasons is because the human body prefers consistency. A varying race pace is something that the body finds too disruptive. Runners who master race pace tend to be those who persistently deliver great PBs in events across a variety of distances. Race pace development will take time and practice.

Although many runners use a heart-rate monitor during training, much of race pace development comes down to a *sense of pace* (or *perceived effort*). This is where we have memorised what a particular pace feels like during training, and can then reproduce this pace under race conditions. As we learnt in the previous section on Long runs, if we avoid race pace practice then how will we know if we could sustain a particular performance in a competition. We may run the risk of starting out in a competition too quickly and then coming a cropper in the second half. The flip side is when we complete a race too slowly; perhaps if we had the courage and confidence in our training then we could have picked our moment in the race, ramped up the pace a little to achieve a good finish time.

Gauging target race pace

When we gauge a target race pace, we have two options. We can either make a rough guess, or use a performance from a distance that we have previously raced. Pete Riegel's formula[1] for calculating race times is considered as one of the more accurate ways of estimating a particular race performance *relative* to a performance from another distance. The formula is as follows:

T2 (Expected time) = T1 x (D2/D1) $^\wedge$ 1.06

Where:

T1 = completion time of a previous race (in minutes)
D1 = distance of a previous race
T2 = calculated expected time of the target race (in minutes)
D2 = distance of the target race
$\wedge$ = the *caret* symbol and signifies exponentiation
1.06 = a constant value that applies to all uses of the formula

Using a 10K performance of 50:30, an estimated half marathon finish time (i.e. T2) could be:

T2 (half marathon time) = 50.5 x (13.1/6.2 *) $^\wedge$ 1.06 = 111.6 minutes

* *10K is approximately 6.2 miles*

A T2 value of 111.6 minutes equates to a half marathon time of 1:51:36.

Based on this estimate, a target half marathon race pace is likely to be around 8.5-minute miles (111.5 minutes/13.1 miles).

Developing race pace

The development of race pace begins with our individual racing aspirations; we can then work our training schedules back from there. For example, if you want to do a 1:45 half marathon, then you need to be able to run at a pace of about 8-minute miles. If your current 10K time is 50:30 minutes (as per the example above), and assuming you have never run for longer than 1-hour then further speed and distance training will be needed to develop speed over a longer distance. As you include 8-minute mile intervals in your longer runs in advance of your target half marathon race (and memorise what that pace feels like), then over time you will condition your body to run at this pace.

TRAINING PRACTICE #6: REST

When we rest we allow our body to adapt to a higher level of fitness and running capability. When we return to training, we should notice an improvement in our performance. There are two types of rest that runners include in their training schedules: rest *days* and rest *periods*:

I. Rest days are included in training schedules to reduce the chances of mental fatigue, exhaustion and injuries. Rest days allow us to replenish our glycogen stocks in time for the next training session. Many runners perceive rest days as a weakness that will have an adverse effect on their performance. The reality is that this is completely not the case. It would take a break of 2-3 weeks from running for any noticeable drop in fitness level to occur. Taking one or two days off from training is not going to significantly impact your fitness level or performance.

The timing and regularity of rest days is largely governed our individual fitness level. Our ability to recover is governed by factors such as age, lifestyle, diet, sleeping patterns, fitness level and training history. Someone new to running would train on one day and then take a rest day but increase that to two consecutive days as they become fitter. An experienced runner may train for at least 5-6 days a week before having a rest day. Elite runners take hardly any rest days at all. They have simply conditioned themselves to recover very quickly in between each training session.

II. Rest periods are breaks from running spanning longer than 1-2 weeks. These kinds of decisions often come about because of circumstances like illness, holidays, work commitments and over-training. Many of these situations are all part of daily life, but over-training in running can be avoided if we train within our physical and aerobic limits. A few aches and pains are normal in any sport, but if you find yourself persistently tired and fatigued then you should cut back on training by about 50% in terms of distance and intensity and limit any increases to around 10% per week. There is no need to completely stop training, unless you have an injury that dictates otherwise. It can take weeks to recover from periods of persistent over-training, but many runners take time out, learn from their experiences and continue to enjoy running.

Many runners take an extended break from running after completing a race like a full marathon. However, it is generally recommended to do some gentle training within 2-3 days after a race to promote the recovery process. Like over-training, a hard stop from running is not always the greatest way of promoting recovery, however strange this may seem.

When returning from a rest period, start from around 60-75% of your normal training routine. For example, if you normally run 35 miles a week, then start back with 20-25 miles a week and aim to get back up to 35 miles within 2-3 weeks.

During periods of rest, your food metabolism will probably slow down and so be sure to modify your food intake, particularly carbohydrates. As we have already discussed, carbohydrates stimulate insulin, a hormone that is responsible for storing fat in the body. Although it is quite normal to gain some extra body weight during periods of rest or low intensity training, we can keep any weight gain down to a minimum by modifying our carbohydrate intake during these periods.

A WORD ON SPORTING INJURIES

It is quite normal to experience a few aches and pains when doing sport. Complications can occur when persistent problems manifest themselves into much bigger problems. We can avoid these situations by adjusting our training schedules. This section briefly discusses the main causes of running related injuries, plus a number of injury prevention and recovery strategies.

Common causes of injury

Running related injuries tend to occur for three main reasons:

I. Over-training, i.e. training beyond our physical limits and not taking adequate recovery and rest.

II. Inadequate stretching, i.e. not warming-up before a training session and not cooling-down afterwards.

III. Bad posture, i.e. slouching when running. An upright posture is an important part of developing an efficient running technique.

Injury prevention

Running related injuries can be prevented by training within our individual physical and aerobic limits, by regularly practising pre and post-training stretching routines plus regular periods of recovery and rest, all subjects that we have already discussed. Cross training and core fitness exercises are also effective ways of developing a strong and upright running posture – more on this in the next chapter.

Injury recovery

The thought of sporting injuries may seem a little daunting and extreme to those new to the sport. Injuries are not all part and parcel of being a runner. The good news is that from my experience, the majority of running related injuries are *muscular* in nature, with the minority being *skeletal* and potentially more serious. Most muscle related injuries can be addressed and permanently resolved. Skeletal related injuries like physical bone and joint problems are more complex and may require help from the medical profession. By comparison, skeletal injuries are quite rare and often come about through accidents rather than overuse. Recovery from an injury is approached in two phases: *Resolution* and *Prevention of re-occurrence*:

I. Resolution – When an injury occurs, it is a good idea to cut back on training volume and intensity. Some injuries will require time out from training, but a complete hard stop from training is not always necessary. Many sporting injuries can be addressed using simple and conservative remedies before engaging the medical profession. Here are a few suggestions that can be practiced at home:

A. Ice and rest for 2-3 days to reduce any muscle swelling – Take a few days off from training and apply an ice-pack to the affected area for 15-20 minutes twice a day. This will help to reduce any muscle swelling around the affected areas.

B. Apply a heat pad to promote recovery – Once any swelling has been reduced, apply a heat-pad to the affected areas also for 15-20 minutes twice a day. This will promote blood supply to the affected areas, the body's greatest natural healer.

C. Gentle stretching – When we gently stretch injured muscles, we start the natural recovery process. It is important that we be *extra* gentle when stretching injured muscles and avoid the risk of putting muscles into *spasm*, another type of muscle injury that can take longer to recover from.

D. Active healing – This is a popular recovery technique that encourages people to remain active whenever possible. Physical injuries don't subside very quickly by sitting down for long periods of time. The quicker we get the blood circulating through the muscles, then the quicker the recovery process begins and the sooner we can get back to training again.

If an injury persists or if you are in any doubt about an injury, then it is wise to consult a qualified sports masseur or a physiotherapist.

II. Prevention of re-occurrence – A full and successful recovery from an injury and a return to the sport is more than possible for most injuries. An effective rehabilitation plan however will help to ensure that an injury does not re-occur again.

A reoccurrence of an injury caused through *over-training* can normally be prevented by reducing weekly mileage and training intensity down to a more manageable level. This will ensure that we are always training within our individual physical and aerobic limits. We can then start to re-develop our running capability in more sustainable increments. A reoccurrence of an injury caused through *bad posture* (for example, lower back pain) can be prevented by developing a more upright posture through core fitness exercises (Chapter 5). Massage and Physiotherapy are useful treatments for promoting the body's natural healing process and may form an integral part of any rehab for more serious and prolonged injuries.

References

1 Riegel, P. (1977)
   Runners World Race Time Predictor
   http://www.runnersworld.co.uk/general/rws-race-time-predictor/1681.html

Chapter 5

Cross Training and Core Fitness

Throughout my time as a runner, I have found that to progress and achieve success in the sport is about more than just running. Indeed, many other good runners that I have known are also those who themselves indulge other sports. On the flip side, I have also found that those who focus on doing just running, often suffer from persistent injuries and disappointing race performances. On that basis, I am a firm believer in promoting core fitness and cross training as complimentary ways of developing both running performance and endurance. As it happens, an increasing number of runners (particularly from the club-runner community) realise the importance of indulging non-running related sports and include them as part of their regular training endeavours for very similar reasons.

When we develop our *core* we are strengthening the abdominals and stomach muscles in and around the mid-section torso area of our body. Our core acts like a centre of gravity and is the part of our body where all sporting movement originates from. When we develop our core fitness in exercises like (e.g.) Swimming, Pilates and Circuits – more on these later – we are simply strengthening our lower back and pelvic regions whilst toning-up our stomach and abdominal muscles. A strong core area will provide an optimum level of general stability when we are running

Many common running-related injuries like (e.g.) lower back pain are known to happen because of a weak core area. What happens in these kinds of situations is that our individual centre of gravity becomes slightly *off-centre* and this causes one side of our body to *over-compensate* for a weaker side, a situation that can create a *muscle-imbalance,* a problem that happens where a muscle or group of muscles on one side of the body will feel more painful than the same muscles on the other side. This feels as if we are expecting one particular side of our body to train harder than the other side.

One way of demonstrating the role of our core in maintaining a good centre of gravity is through a quick experiment using the *Quadriceps* stretch from Chapter 2 (page 31).

Using the *sideways* image as a guide, perform the quadriceps stretch as you normally would do by engaging your abdominals and stomach muscles. Then, standing with one hand on a wall just in case you lose your balance, perform the stretch again but this time relax your core area. What you may find is that as you slouch, it is more difficult to maintain a good balance with a fixed centre of gravity. If you were to then re-engage your core, you should return to a more upright and stable posture. A similar kind of scenario happens when we run. If we run with a slouched posture and a shifting centre of gravity, the result is that other parts or sides of our body will have to over-compensate. The result can be muscle imbalances and other injuries.

Resolving problems caused through muscle-imbalances can be challenging and time consuming. What many runners do under these circumstances is to cut back on training mileage and intensity, gently stretch, apply a heat pad to the affected areas to enhance blood supply, and possibly request the help from a sports masseur or physiotherapist to free up any stiff muscles. Then as a next step they may embark on regular core fitness exercises to *re-centre* their core and prevent further muscle-imbalance issues from returning again in the future. That may sound somewhat simplistic, but it is an approach that is known to work well over a period of time.

Runners are reminded that despite the benefits and enjoyment of playing other sports, cross training and core fitness exercises are not generally considered as substitutes for running training. During periods of focused training like, for example, training for an important race, at least 80% of your training must be running related. To become good at running you still need to build your base mileage and speed performance using the techniques outlined in Chapter 4.

CROSS TRAINING AND CORE FITNESS EXERCISES

The remainder of this chapter is split up into five sections (I-IV) that consider some extra-curricular activities that are well known to the running community. They are cycling, swimming, gym training, Pilates and circuit training:

I. Cycling is a popular non-impact exercise highly relevant to runners. When we cycle, our hip, knee and ankle joints are *rotated* instead of *impacted*. Cycling is also another aerobic sport that exercises our heart and lungs in a similar way to running and is therefore ideal for maintaining and developing our VO2 Max. Both running and cycling at (e.g.) 80% MHR will have a similar effect on our cardiovascular system. Due to its low impact on the joints, cycling is enables a faster recovery. Some runners develop their core fitness by riding a mountain bike (with studded tyres) on the road. The increased tyre-resistance on a road makes mountain bike cycling just that little bit harder.

II. Swimming is a popular exercise for runners because it develops the core and upper body muscles. This kind of strength training is useful for maintaining an upright posture. Swimming also helps stretch out the body and is considered a highly effective way of keeping injuries to a minimum, particularly in the lower back regions.

III. Gym training – Regular gym attendance is great for building general fitness. Any form of weight training, whether it be free-weights or the various weight-focused machines, are all good for developing general muscle strength and shedding body fat. The rowing machines, step machines and cross trainer are all low-impact forms of exercise great for building core fitness. Many gyms have an area allocated for people who like to use a stability ball for developing core strength.

IV. Pilates is a form of physical fitness developed in the 20th Century by Joseph Pilates, a German physical-culturist. The focus of Pilates training focuses on building muscle flexibility, strength and endurance in areas such as the legs, abdominals, arms, hips, and back. The practice of Pilates places a high emphasis on spinal and pelvic alignment, deep breathing, and developing a strong core as well as improving physical coordination and balance. Pilates also has the additional benefit of being able to relax the body in such a way that allows us to move more elegantly (suppleness). Much of Pilates practice is focused around strengthening our core areas to ensure a correct and healthy spinal curvature.

It is beyond the scope of this book to discuss Pilates in any great level of detail. Any reader who wishes to try their hand at Pilates is encouraged to locate a Pilates' class in their local area and have a go. Like most sports, many Pilates' sessions are categorised into Beginners, Intermediate and Advanced. The difference between each of the three categories focuses around technical difficulty; some Pilates moves are quite complex and will take some practice. The feedback around Pilates from within the running community has been generally positive.

Despite the growing popularity of Pilates as a regular form of exercise amongst everyday people, a systematic review[1] did *not* conclude that regular Pilates practice was a general and effective way of addressing lower back pain across the board. From our perspective, this evidential finding doesn't pose a major problem simply because I am not aware of any silver bullets for preventing running related injuries. Many of the suggestions contained in this book are simply designed to *reduce* the risk of injury through structured running training. This can only really happen if we train within our *physical* and *aerobic* limits.

V. Circuit training (or *circuits*) is when you go around and do different exercises for a fixed amount of time and then move on to the next one straight away. You continue doing this for a fixed amount of time before taking a recovery period before doing it all over again. The practical part of this section includes a circuits' session consisting of 14 well known fitness exercises. Before going into the details of each exercise, *three* levels of example training programmes are presented that readers can choose from depending on their general fitness level or their previous experience of practicing circuits.

A *set* is a continuous run of all of the 14 exercises back to back. All exercises are required to be performed regardless of level. The differences between each level focus around *exercise duration, recovery period* and *total number of sets*:

Level 1 circuits – 2 sets with a 5-minute recovery

- Each exercise is performed continuously for 30 seconds.
- A 30-second recovery is allowed in between each exercise.
- Repeat the set after a 5-minute recovery period.
- Total training duration is 33 minutes (excluding warm-up and cool-down).

Level 2 circuits – 3 sets with a 4-minute recovery

- Each exercise is performed continuously for 45 seconds.
- A 15-second recovery is allowed in between each exercise.
- Take a 4-minute recovery between each of the 3 sets.
- Total training duration is 50 minutes (excluding warm-up and cool-down).

Level 3 circuits – 3 sets with a 3-minute recovery

- Each exercise is performed continuously for 1-minute.
- A 20-second recovery is allowed in between each exercise.
- Take a 3-minute recovery between each of the 3 sets.
- Total training duration is 62 minutes (excluding warm-up and cool-down).

Useful tips for when practicing circuits:

- Pace yourself. Try and hold the exercise, or complete as many reps of each exercise as is possible for the total interval duration without stopping.
- Always try and engage your core areas by holding in your abdominals and stomach muscles. While you do this, try and breathe normally – this may take some practice but it is an important part of core development.

- Take advantage of the recovery period and prepare for the next exercise in the set.

- Be determined – circuit training is not supposed to be easy.

Before starting a circuits session, gently jog for 3-5 minutes before completing your usual warm-up routine. Reset your stopwatch.

The first exercise in the set is **Press-ups** (next page).

1. Press-ups

Fig. 1.1 Raised position

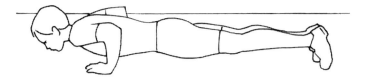

Fig. 1.2 Lowered position

Purpose: To develop the upper body, biceps and the core areas.

Technique: Start in the raised position (Fig 1.1) with your arms straight and knees and toes together and with your back straight. Your hands should be slightly wider than shoulder width apart. Then bend your arms and lower your body to the point where your body is just off the ground (Fig 1.2). After about half a second, raise your body back up to the raised position (Fig. 1.1).

2. Tricep push-ups

Fig. 2.1 Raised position

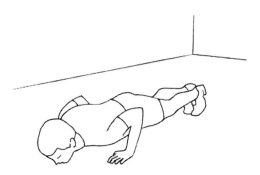

Fig. 2.2 Lowered position

Purpose: To develop the upper body, triceps and the core areas.

Technique: Start in the raised position (Fig 2.1) with your arms straight and knees and toes together and with your back straight. Your hands should be in line with your shoulders. Then bend your arms and lower your body to the point where your body is just off the ground (Fig 2.2). After about half a second, raise your body back up to the raised position (Fig. 2.1).

3. Squat thrusts

Fig. 3.1 Squat position

Fig. 3.2 Raised press-up position

Purpose: To develop the upper body, biceps and the core areas.

Technique: Start in the squat position (Fig 3.1) with your arms straight. From the squat position, push your feet back into the raised press-up position keeping your back straight (Fig. 3.2). After a split second, return to the squat position (Fig. 3.1).

4. Sit ups

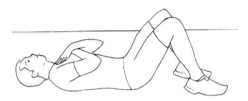

Fig. 4.1 Resting position

Fig 4.2 Upright position

Purpose: To develop the core areas – stomach and abdominals.

Technique: Lie down on the floor with both your knees bent. Cross your hands across the chest (Fig. 4.1.). Engage your core and raise your shoulders from the ground (Fig. 4.2.). Keep your hands on the chest at all times. Keeping your core engaged, gently return your upper body back to the resting position (Fig. 4.1).

5. Star jumps

Purpose: To strengthen the shoulders, adductors and the core areas.

Technique: Begin by jumping up and down on the spot. Then start to spread your arms and legs in synchronisation whilst continuing to jump.

6. Squats

Purpose: To strengthen the hamstrings, glutes and the core areas.

Technique: Stand with your feet shoulder width apart. Place your arms out in front and squat down whilst keeping your toes facing outwards. Try and keep your back straight and look ahead.

7. Leg raise

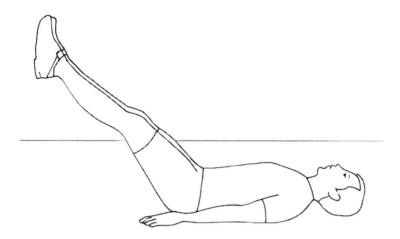

Purpose: To strengthen the hamstrings, glutes, quadriceps and the core areas.

Technique: Lay on the ground with both of your legs straight. Raise both of your legs from the ground to 45 degrees and then hold for the duration of the interval. Avoid arching your back by pushing your lower back towards the floor. At the end of the interval time, gently lower your legs back to the floor.

The other alternative for this exercise is to rotate the feet and the legs in a *figure of 8* whilst keeping your legs raised.

8. Scissors

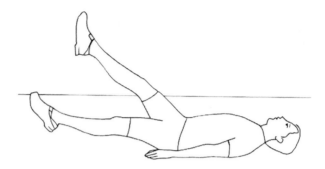

Purpose: To strengthen the hamstrings, glutes, quadriceps and the core areas.

Technique: Lay on the ground with both of your legs straight. Raise both legs off the ground slightly and hold. Then raise one leg slightly and then lower again, and then change sides slowly alternating. Your legs must not touch the ground throughout the exercise.

9. Burpees

Fig. 9.1 Standing position   Fig. 9.2 Squat position

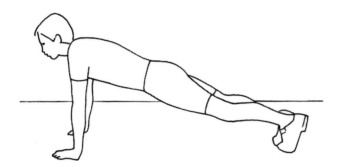

Fig. 9.3 Raised press-up position

continued ...

9. Burpees (continued)

Fig. 9.4 Squat position   Fig. 9.5 Standing position

Purpose: A good all round exercise aimed at developing both the lower and upper body and the core areas.

Technique: Stand up straight with your hands in the air (Fig. 9.1). Then squat down with your arms straight (Fig. 9.2). From the squat position, push your feet back into a raised press-up position (Fig. 9.3). After a split second, return to the squat position (Fig 9.4) and then stand up straight and put your hands in the air (Fig. 9.5).

10. Fingers to toes

Purpose: To strengthen the core areas and stretch the glutes and hamstrings.

Technique: Lie on the ground with both your legs straight. Keeping your legs straight, raise them both to 90 degrees and simultaneously bring your hands up towards the toes. With your core engaged, aim to touch your toes with the tips of your fingers for a split second before relaxing. Keep your legs up at 90 degrees. Rest for a second and then repeat.

11. The plank

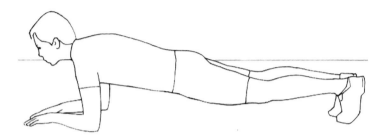

Purpose: A good all round exercise aimed at developing both the lower body and upper body and the core areas.

Technique: Lie on the floor and support your body with your forearms flat on the ground. Raise your stomach and support your body using your toes. Hold your core at all times and breathe normally. Always keep your back straight. Avoid letting your lower back sag or drop to the floor.

12. Kneeling arm and leg reach

Purpose: To stretch the arms and legs whilst maintaining a good balance by engaging the core.

Technique: Stand on all fours and push one arm away. Then push your opposite leg away. Keep the raised arm and opposite leg both parallel to the floor and ensure that you always look towards the floor whilst you are doing the exercise. Hold for 5 seconds and then swap sides.

13. Bent knees

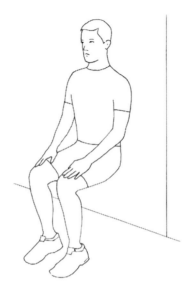

Purpose: To strengthen the quadriceps and the core areas.

Technique: Lean against the wall and lower your body so that your knees are bent at 90 degrees. Point your feet straight ahead and keep your knees a hip's distance apart. Lean back against the wall and look straight ahead. Engage your core areas whilst breathing normally and relax your shoulders.

14. Hip flexors

Purpose: To strengthen the quadriceps and hip flexors. This is similar to post-training exercise #5 from Chapter 4 (page 67).

Technique: Stand upright and step back with one foot nearly as far as the leg will reach. Squat down slightly until your knee is just off the ground keeping your body upright. Use your arms to maintain balance and posture and keep looking straight ahead. Hold the stretch for a split second, stand up straight again and then alternate with the opposite leg.

The more difficult alternative is to quickly alternate each side by striding forwards and backwards on the spot with each leg.

That completes one set of circuits. It is now time to start your recovery of either 3, 4 or 5 minutes as per your training level and prepare yourself for the next set (Level 1 has *two* sets; Levels 2 and 3 each have *three* sets).

After completing your circuits' session, remember to do your post-training cool-down routine of stretching, re-hydration and eating within an hour.

References

1   Wells, C; Kolt, G.S; Marshall, P; Hill, B; Bialocerkowski, A (2013)
    *Effectiveness of Pilates exercise in treating people with chronic low
    back pain: A systematic review of systematic reviews*
    BMC Medical Research Methodology 13: 7

Chapter 6

Race Training from 5K up to Half Marathon

This chapter covers the subject of preparing and training for a competitive road race. Three example structured training plans are presented that take runners with no previous racing experience from the 5K distance (Schedule 1) up to 10K (Schedule 2) and then half marathon (Schedule 3). Readers can gauge their own individual level of running experience and choose which of the three schedules they would like to start from. For example, a runner experienced in the 5K distance could either aim to improve their 5K time, or maybe start from the 10K schedule and progress from there. A beginner who has never run before (like someone who started out in running by following Chapter 2) would be advised to start from a simple 5K race (Schedule 1) and work their way from there. At the end of each of the schedules there are some ideas on how to improve your performance in that distance. You may find these suggestions useful if you are looking to improve your performance in a particular distance.

Throughout this book we have discussed a number of training practices ranging from *Recovery*, *VO2 Max*, *Threshold*, *Hills*, *Long runs*, *Race pace* and *Rest* in Chapter 4 plus some further ideas around core fitness and cross training in Chapter 5. The training schedules in this chapter incorporate many of these ideas and principles either directly or indirectly in various guises. Therefore, to keep things simple, I have created *four* categories that will appear at the beginning of each schedule to articulate the purpose of each plan: *Endurance and stamina*, *Speed*, *Recovery and rest* and *Race pace*. If you want to become good at running competitions, then it is a good idea to focus on these four areas.

Runners are encouraged to progress through the schedules one by one in a way that is both realistic and sustainable. You will be far happier with your race performances if you gradually work your way through the schedules towards your target racing distance. The trick with successful training is to build running capability gently and avoid cutting corners.

Novice runners or those with a limited experience of racing are discouraged from skipping this chapter and going straight into Chapter 7 and doing full marathon training. They are encouraged instead to begin their training endeavours at the 5K distance and work their way through the 10K and half marathon distances first. By taking this approach, runners will gently build their stamina and core fitness and keep injuries at bay. This will also result in better and more enjoyable race performances and not to mention some longevity in the sport.

Getting the most from the training schedules

The three schedules are only a training guide and are by no means definitive. They simply serve to provide runners with a useful starting point in their training endeavours and racing aspirations. If a schedule looks too difficult, then runners are encouraged to try an easier schedule and work their way up through the distances. Runners may find the following points useful:

I. Running development is down to the individual – Each and every one us will develop our racing capability in our own way and at our own pace. Our bodies will adapt accordingly as and when the time is right.

II. Racing distance development should be sustainable – Runners are encouraged to develop a sustained performance in a particular distance before moving to the next distance. It is fine to start running with the aspiration of going straight into a full marathon (Chapter 7), but this book doesn't recommend that approach.

III. Racing ability takes time to develop – A training schedule is no guarantee of a certain performance level after the first attempt. Training plans need to be worked on and amended where necessary. Skills like focus, persistence and determination are critical for any investment in training to be fully realised. Without those skills, a training schedule in its own right is only partly useful.

IV. Race training distance is all a matter of choice – It is a matter of individual choice how far through the schedules that a runner wishes to go. Some runners may stop at 10K and make that particular distance their specialty, whereas others may work their way up to Chapter 7 and do well at full marathon level.

Each of the schedules is designed to be typically harder than the previous one. The training distances get longer and the training intensity level will increase. As we progress into the 10K distance, there is a greater emphasis on developing race pace.

Can the schedules be amended?
Given the highly subjective nature of training schedules, it is likely that many readers will, over time, create their own plans to include (e.g.) activities like cross training and core fitness that were outlined in Chapter 5. This is fine, but when you are in periods of focused running training, at least 80% of your training should be running related. The following elements within each of the schedules must remain in place wherever possible:

Long runs – The development of base mileage is a critical part of being able to run over distance for extended periods time (e.g., 60-90 minutes or more). Runners often do their long runs on a Sunday morning simply because this is the time of the week when races are normally scheduled and is a great way of preparing for a race.

Speed sessions – These are critical for developing running performance. It is hard to develop speed purely on the back of long runs. Speed sessions are normally done around mid-week in time for a rest day before a long run on a Sunday. This is generally good practice.

Run sessions – Runners training for a race should aim to do at least one or two easy or steady runs each week as per the schedule. This keeps the core of the training focused on running related activities.

Rest days – Rest days are normally taken at the beginning of the week after a long run on a Sunday, and towards the end of the week after a few days of high-intensity training. This is good practice and beginners in particular are well advised to adopt this approach.

If, on the other hand, we were to make changes to a training schedule and include things like cross training or core fitness exercises, the following guidelines are worth considering:

Rest days – Anyone with a good level of fitness can if they choose miss a rest day and maybe go cycling, swimming or visit the gym. It is however still good practice to take things gently on (e.g.) a Monday, the day after a long run. The ability to recover is a key part of successful training and must not be scrimped on, regardless of how fit we are. Injuries can sometimes lurk and then make themselves known at times when we least expect them too. This is a risk not worth taking and is why runners are encouraged to take regular rest days.

Cross training – Some runners may (e.g.) go cycling on a Saturday instead of doing a run. They may cycle for an hour or maybe an hour and a half on the day before doing their long run.

Core fitness – The inclusion of weekly circuits or hill training in advance of a hilly race are all good training tactics. These are best done mid-week between Tuesday and Thursday either side of a rest period.

> Racing teaches us to challenge ourselves. It teaches us to push beyond where we thought we could go. It helps us to find out what we are made of. This is what we do. This is what it's all about – *PattiSue Plumer, Former USA Olympian*

Age-related race performances

Age-related performances are a good way of putting all race participants on a level playing field, irrespective of age or gender. They allow us to compare our individual race times to other runners and see where we are in terms of the current global standard for our age and gender. Information about race performances is provided by the World Masters Athletics (WMA).

Some race organisers will include this information on their results summaries against each competitor's finish time.

Age-related calculators are available on-line, the one by Howard Grubb[1] being one of the most well known. For example, a male of 35 years of age who completed a 5K race in 21:30 will have an age-graded score of 59.95% and an age-graded time of 21:03. An age-graded *score* (e.g., 59.95%) is the ratio of the approximate world-record time based on your age and gender divided by your race finish time. An age-graded *time* (e.g., 21:03) is your adjusted race finish time based on an open division participant incorporating a factor for age and gender. Many runners use this information to see how well they are performing in races.

Calculating and gauging a target race pace

As we progress into Schedules 2 and 3 and look at the 10K and half marathon distances, it is useful to know your potential 10K and half marathon finish times so that you can gauge your ideal race pace. This is because you will be expected to complete a portion of your longer runs (scheduled for a Sunday) at your target race pace, a practice that will probably lead to a better race performance.

In Chapter 4 when we looked at how to develop *race pace*, we used Pete Riegel's formula[2] for calculating race times. For the purposes of simplicity, we will use a *5K* performance from Schedule 1 to estimate a *10K* performance for Schedule 2, and a 10K performance to estimate a *half marathon* finish time for Schedule 3. Pete Riegel's formula is as follows:

T2 (Expected time) = T1 x (D2/D1) ^ 1.06

Where:

    T1 = completion time of a previous race (in minutes)
    D1 = distance of a previous race
    T2 = calculated expected time of the target race (in minutes)
    D2 = distance of the target race
    ^   = the *caret* symbol and signifies exponentiation
    1.06 = a constant value that applies to all uses of the formula

Using a 5K performance of 29.5 minutes, an estimated 10K finish time (i.e. T2) could be:

T2 (10K time) = 29.5 x (10/5) ^ 1.06 = 61.5 minutes

A T2 value of 61.5 minutes equates to a 10K time of 1:01:30.

Using an estimated 10K time of 1:01:30 for gauging our race pace in Schedule 2, we would be looking at running at a pace of just over 6-minute per kilometre. As you continue to work through Schedule 2, and maybe reduce your 10K time to (e.g.) 50 minutes, an estimated half marathon time would be:

T2 (half marathon time) = 50 x (13.1/6.2 *) ^ 1.06 = **111.6 minutes**

* *10K is approximately 6.2 miles*

A T2 value of 110.5 minutes equates to a half marathon time of 1:50:30.

If we were to then use this half marathon estimate of 1:50:30 for gauging our race pace in Schedule 3, then our minute per mile pace during the race pace portion of the longer runs would be just under 8.5-minute per mile.

Note that these values are only estimates. They do still however provide a reasonable starting point for developing race pace, a critical part of being successful in race competitions.

Terminology used in the schedules

Each of the training schedules will use a common way of expressing the training requirements of a particular session. The following is a list of *example* training sessions (in **bold**) along with an appropriate explanation.

---

5 miles Easy
This is a 5 mile run at a pace of 65-70% MHR, i.e. a pace that is slightly faster than conversational pace.

---

7 miles Steady
This is a 7 mile run at between 70-80% MHR, i.e. a pace where you can say about one sentence before being out of breath.

1-hour cross training
This is spending 1-hour doing some of the extra-curricular activities from Chapter 5.

2 sets of 30 seconds fast with 30 seconds recovery (x8)
4 minutes recovery between each set
This is 30 seconds fast followed by a 30-second recovery done a total of eight times back to back – this is one *set*. This is followed by a 4-minute recovery jog where the set is then repeated.

6 miles Steady
Include 2 x 6-minute threshold intervals
4 minutes recovery between each set
This is a 6 mile run at a steady pace of 70-80% MHR. During that 6 mile run you will do a 6-minute run at threshold pace followed by a 4-minute recovery at a steady pace. This is followed by another 6-minute threshold run. Ideally you should aim to spend the first 10-15 minutes of the run warming up before starting the first threshold interval.

3 x 6 minutes @ threshold pace
3 minutes recovery between each threshold
This is three 6-minute runs at threshold pace with a 3-minute recovery jog between each threshold.

RACE TRAINING SCHEDULES

Readers now have the choice as to which of the three training schedules they are comfortable with starting from. A summary is given below.

Training Schedule	Experience level
Schedule 1: 5K Sub 35 minutes	30-minute Easy run non-stop
Schedule 2: 10K Sub 1-hour	45-minute Steady run non-stop
Schedule 3: Half Marathon Sub 1:40	60-minute Steady run non-stop

Before and after each of the schedules, remember to do your warm-up and cool-down routines. You should be good at this by now!

SCHEDULE 1: 5K Sub 35 minutes

The following 8-week training plan is aimed at someone who can run non-stop for at least 30 minutes at an easy pace. This is likely to be someone who started out as a beginner in running and may have followed the training plans in Chapter 2. This schedule is designed to prepare you to complete a 5K non-stop in a time of under 35 minutes. Some guidelines for further improving your 5K time are given after the schedule. A summary of the four training categories is as follows:

Endurance and stamina – The first 4 out of the 8 weeks will include three runs that focus on developing 3 miles at easy pace up to 5 miles at a steady pace. This is good initial base mileage and stamina training. The second half of the schedule includes a weekly easy and steady paced run that develops further base mileage up to 7 miles. One of the three runs from the first half of the schedule is also changed into a combination of both distance and speed intervals.

Speed – One weekly speed session is introduced that develops short but fast intervals starting from 30 seconds increasing to 45 seconds with equal amounts of recovery. During the second half of the schedule that will increase to 60-second intervals with an equal recovery time. This kind of training is similar to Level 1 VO2 Max in Chapter 4 which is ideal for developing speed over shorter distances like 5K. The second half of the schedule will include an element of speed practice as part of a steady run. Further speed and stamina can (if you choose) be developed by running over an undulating course.

Recovery and rest – Running training is limited to only 4 days a week with the remaining 3 days a week as rest. The tapering off period in Week 8 encourages a reduced training time that still includes an element of high intensity training in advance of race day.

Race pace – For beginners, the development of race pace is not a major focus for this particular schedule. For now, you should aim to run at a pace that is comfortably fast. We will use your 5K race time as a basis for developing a good 10K time in Schedule 2.

SCHEDULE 1: 8-Week 5K Sub 35 minutes	
WEEK 1	
Monday	Rest day
Tuesday	4 miles Easy
Wednesday	2 sets of 30 seconds fast with 30 seconds recovery (x8) 4 minutes recovery between each set
Thursday	Rest day
Friday	4 miles Easy
Saturday	Rest day
Sunday	4 miles Easy
WEEK 2	
Monday	Rest day
Tuesday	4 miles Easy
Wednesday	2 sets of 30 seconds with fast 30 seconds recovery (x10) 4 minutes recovery between each set
Thursday	Rest day
Friday	4 miles Easy
Saturday	Rest day
Sunday	5 miles Steady
WEEK 3	
Monday	Rest day
Tuesday	4 miles Easy
Wednesday	2 sets of 45 seconds with fast 45 seconds recovery (x8) 4 minutes recovery between each set
Thursday	Rest day
Friday	5 miles Easy
Saturday	Rest day
Sunday	5 miles Steady
WEEK 4	
Monday	Rest day
Tuesday	4 miles Easy
Wednesday	Rest day
Thursday	2 sets of 45 seconds with fast 45 seconds recovery (x10) 4 minutes recovery between each set
Friday	5 miles Easy
Saturday	Rest day
Sunday	6 miles Steady

WEEK 5	
Monday	Rest day
Tuesday	5 miles Steady Include 2 sets of 4 x 2 minutes fast with a 1-minute recovery
Wednesday	Rest day
Thursday	60 seconds fast with 60 seconds recovery (x6) 4 minutes recovery between each set
Friday	4 miles Easy
Saturday	Rest day
Sunday	6 miles Steady

WEEK 6	
Monday	Rest day
Tuesday	6 miles Steady Include 2 sets of 6 x 2 minutes fast with a 1-minute recovery
Wednesday	Rest day
Thursday	2 sets of 60 seconds fast with 60 seconds recovery (x8) 4 minutes recovery between each set
Friday	4 miles Easy
Saturday	Rest day
Sunday	6 miles Steady

WEEK 7	
Monday	Rest day
Tuesday	6 miles Steady Include 2 sets of 8 x 2 minutes fast with a 1-minute recovery
Wednesday	Rest day
Thursday	4 miles Easy
Friday	2 sets of 45 seconds fast with 45 seconds recovery (x10) 4 minutes recovery between each set
Saturday	Rest day
Sunday	7 miles Steady

WEEK 8 – Race Week	
Monday	Rest day
Tuesday	3 miles Easy
Wednesday	2 sets of 60 seconds fast with 60 seconds recovery (x6) 4 minutes recovery between each set
Thursday	Rest day
Friday	4 miles Steady
Saturday	Rest day
Sunday	RACE DAY

Guidelines around further reducing your 5K time

Runners who have followed Schedule 1 and would like to further reduce their 5K time may like to continue with the above schedules but gently introduce the following adjustments:

- Increase respective run times by around 30-50%, e.g. a 4 mile easy or steady run would increase to around 5-6 miles.

- Increase the amount of speed training by doing 90 seconds fast with a 3-minute recovery. Ideally and as you get good at practicing speed, you should be looking to use both the dedicated and combined speed sessions to improve your *VO2 Max* whilst at the same time reducing your recovery time.

- Replace a rest day with a 4-5 mile steady run.

SCHEDULE 2: 10K Sub 1-hour

The following 8-week training plan is a follow-on from Schedule 2 and is aimed at someone who can run non-stop for at least 45 minutes at a steady pace and is aspiring to run a 10K race non-stop in under 1-hour. Before you progress, and using Pete Riegel's race performance formula[2], it is worth estimating your 10K finish time and target race pace (a worked example of Pete Riegel's formula can be found on page 90 and pages 121–122). This could be based on your fastest 5K finish time from Schedule 1, or another distance that you may have previously raced. This is useful to know in advance of weeks 6 and 7 where you will be doing a portion of your long run at race pace. A summary of the four training categories is as follows:

Endurance and stamina – The first 4 out of the 8 weeks will include three runs that focus on developing 4 miles at easy pace up to 7 miles at a steady pace. This is good base mileage and stamina training. The second half of the schedule includes a weekly easy and steady paced run that develops further base mileage up to 9 miles. One of the three runs from the first half of the schedule is also changed into a combination of both distance and speed intervals.

Speed – One weekly speed session is scheduled between weeks 1 through to 4 that develop short but fast intervals starting from 60 seconds increasing to 90 seconds with equal amounts of recovery. The speed sessions in the second half of the schedule focus on longer 2-minute intervals with a 1-minute recovery time. The second half of the schedule will include a threshold element as part of a steady run to further develop speed but over a longer distance.

Recovery and rest – Running training is limited to only 4 days a week with the remaining 3 days a week as rest. The tapering off period in Week 8 encourages a reduced training time that still includes an element of high intensity training in advance of race day.

Race pace – During weeks 6 and 7, the longer steady run on the Sunday will require the last 2-3 miles to be completed at your target 10K race pace.

SCHEDULE 2: 8-Week 10K Sub 1-hour	
WEEK 1	
Monday	Rest day
Tuesday	4 miles Steady
Wednesday	2 sets of 60 seconds fast with 60 seconds recovery (x6) 3 minutes recovery between each set
Thursday	Rest day
Friday	5 miles Easy
Saturday	Rest day
Sunday	5 miles Steady
WEEK 2	
Monday	Rest day
Tuesday	4 miles Steady
Wednesday	2 sets of 60 seconds fast with 60 seconds recovery (x8) 3 minutes recovery between each set
Thursday	Rest day
Friday	5 miles Easy
Saturday	Rest day
Sunday	5 miles Steady
WEEK 3	
Monday	Rest day
Tuesday	5 miles Easy
Wednesday	2 sets of 90 seconds fast with 90 seconds recovery (x5) 3 minutes recovery between each set

continued...

Thursday	Rest day
Friday	5 miles Easy
Saturday	Rest day
Sunday	6 miles Steady
WEEK 4	
Monday	Rest day
Tuesday	5 miles Easy
Wednesday	Rest day
Thursday	2 sets of 90 seconds fast with 90 seconds recovery (x7) 3 minutes recovery between each set
Friday	5 miles Easy
Saturday	Rest day
Sunday	7 miles Steady
WEEK 5	
Monday	Rest day
Tuesday	6 miles Steady Include 2 x 6-minute threshold intervals 4 minutes recovery between each threshold
Wednesday	Rest day
Thursday	2 sets of 2 minutes fast with a 1-minute recovery (x4) 3 minutes recovery between each set
Friday	5 miles Easy
Saturday	Rest day
Sunday	7 miles Steady
WEEK 6	
Monday	Rest day
Tuesday	7 miles Steady Include 2 x 7-minute threshold intervals 4 minutes recovery between each threshold
Wednesday	Rest day
Thursday	2 sets of 2 minutes fast with a 1-minute recovery (x5) 3 minutes recovery between each set
Friday	5 miles Easy
Saturday	Rest day
Sunday	8 miles Steady – last 2 miles at your target 10K race pace

WEEK 7	
Monday	Rest day
Tuesday	7 miles Steady Include 2 x 7-minute threshold intervals 3 minutes recovery between each threshold
Wednesday	Rest day
Thursday	5 miles Easy
Friday	2 sets of 2 minutes fast with a 1-minute recovery (x6) 3 minutes recovery
Saturday	Rest day
Sunday	9 miles Steady – last 3 miles at your target 10K race pace
WEEK 8 – Race Week	
Monday	Rest day
Tuesday	3 miles Easy
Wednesday	2 sets of 60 seconds fast with 60 seconds recovery (x6) 4 minutes recovery between each set
Thursday	Rest day
Friday	4 miles Steady
Saturday	Rest day
Sunday	RACE DAY

Guidelines around further reducing your 10K time

Runners who have followed Schedule 2 and would like to further reduce their time may like to continue with the above schedule, but make the following general adjustments:

- Increase respective run times by around 30-50%,
  e.g. a 6 mile steady run would increase to around 8-9 miles.

- Increase the running intervals in the speed sessions, i.e.
  try and run for 3 minutes fast with a 2-minute recovery, or increase the threshold pace in the weekly steady run up to 8, 9 or even 10 minutes.

- Replace a Rest day with a 4-5 mile steady run.

SCHEDULE 3: Half Marathon Sub 1:40

The following 12-week training plan is aimed at someone who can run non-stop for at least 60 minutes at a steady pace and is aspiring to run a half marathon non-stop in a time under 1:40 hours. Before you progress, and using Pete Riegel's race performance formula[2], it is worth estimating your half marathon finish time (page 122). This could be based on your fastest 10K finish time from Schedule 2, or another distance that you may have pre-viously raced. A summary of the four training categories is as follows:

Endurance and stamina – Base mileage is developed from 4 miles up to 12 miles during the first five weeks using varying combina tions of easy and steady runs. Week 5 is a quiet week. During weeks 6 through to 10 you will complete a 6 or 7 mile steady run in the week. Two of your long runs (scheduled for a Sunday) will be 15 miles and are useful for developing further base mileage. During the tapering off period in weeks (11 and 12), running distance is reduced to provide adequate recovery in advance of race day.

Speed – During weeks 1 through to 4, the emphasis will be on doing short bursts of 2 and 3-minute intervals as a way of developing speed. Then from weeks 5 through to 10, the focus shifts to doing threshold training as a way of developing speed over a sustained distance. During the tapering off period in weeks (11 and 12), speed sessions consist of shorter bursts to keep the intensity high in advance of race day.

Recovery and rest – An easy run is scheduled for every Monday straight after a longer run on the Sunday. This will enable ample recovery in time for a speed session on either the Tuesday or a Wednesday. Two rest days are scheduled for each week where week 6 is a quiet week.

Race pace – Half marathon target race pace intervals are included at the tail end of the Sunday long run from Week 7 and onwards. This provides an opportunity to develop race pace in advance of race day.

Schedule 3 begins on the next page.

SCHEDULE 3: 12-Week Half marathon Sub 1:40	
WEEK 1	
Monday	5 miles Easy
Tuesday	2 sets of 2 minutes fast with a 1-minute recovery (x5) 2 minutes recovery between each set
Wednesday	Rest day
Thursday	5 miles Steady
Friday	Rest day
Saturday	1-hour cross training
Sunday	8 miles Steady
WEEK 2	
Monday	5 miles Easy
Tuesday	2 sets of 2 minutes fast with a 1-minute recovery (x6) 2 minutes recovery between each set
Wednesday	Rest day
Thursday	6 miles Steady
Friday	Rest day
Saturday	1-hour cross training
Sunday	9 miles Steady
WEEK 3	
Monday	4 miles Easy
Tuesday	2 sets of 3 minutes fast with 2 minutes recovery (x4) 2 minutes recovery between each set
Wednesday	Rest day
Thursday	7 miles Steady
Friday	Rest day
Saturday	1.5 hours cross training
Sunday	11 miles Steady
WEEK 4	
Monday	4 miles Easy
Tuesday	2 sets of 3 minutes fast with 2 minutes recovery (x5) 2 minutes recovery between each set
Wednesday	Rest day
Thursday	7 miles Steady
Friday	Rest day
Saturday	1.5 hours cross training
Sunday	12 miles Steady

WEEK 5	
Monday	4 miles Easy
Tuesday	3 x 6 minutes @ threshold pace 3 minutes recovery between each threshold
Wednesday	Rest day
Thursday	5 miles Steady
Friday	Rest day
Saturday	1-hour cross training
Sunday	8 miles Steady
WEEK 6	
Monday	4 miles Easy
Tuesday	4 x 6 minutes @ threshold pace 3 minutes recovery between each threshold
Wednesday	Rest day
Thursday	7 miles Steady
Friday	Rest day
Saturday	1-hour cross training
Sunday	12 miles Steady
WEEK 7	
Monday	4 miles Easy
Tuesday	Rest day
Wednesday	4 x 7 minutes @ threshold pace 3 minutes recovery between each threshold
Thursday	Rest day
Friday	8 miles Steady
Saturday	1.5 hours cross training
Sunday	15 miles Steady – last 5 miles @ half marathon pace
WEEK 8	
Monday	4 miles Easy
Tuesday	Rest day
Wednesday	3 x 9 minutes @ threshold pace 3 minutes recovery between each threshold
Thursday	Rest day
Friday	6 miles Steady
Saturday	1-hour cross training
Sunday	9 miles Steady – last 3 miles @ half marathon pace

WEEK 9	
Monday	4 miles Easy
Tuesday	Rest day
Wednesday	3 x 10 minutes @ threshold pace 3 minutes recovery between each threshold
Thursday	Rest day
Friday	7 miles Steady
Saturday	1.5 hours cross training
Sunday	15 miles Steady – last 5 miles @ half marathon pace
WEEK 10	
Monday	4 miles Easy
Tuesday	Rest day
Wednesday	3 x 11 minutes @ threshold pace 3 minutes recovery between each threshold
Thursday	Rest day
Friday	8 miles Steady
Saturday	1.5 hours cross training
Sunday	12 miles Steady – last 4 miles @ half marathon pace
WEEK 11	
Monday	4 miles Easy
Tuesday	2 sets of 90 seconds fast with 60 seconds recovery (x8) 3 minutes recovery between each set
Wednesday	Rest day
Thursday	5 miles Steady
Friday	Rest day
Saturday	1-hour cross training
Sunday	9 miles Steady – last 3 miles @ half marathon pace
WEEK 12 – Race Week	
Monday	4 miles Easy
Tuesday	2 sets of 90 seconds fast with 60 seconds recovery (x6) 3 minutes recovery between each set
Wednesday	6 miles Steady
Thursday	Rest day
Friday	5 miles Steady – last 3 miles @ half marathon pace
Saturday	Rest day
Sunday	RACE DAY

Guidelines around further reducing your half marathon time

Runners who have followed Schedule 3 and would like to further reduce their half marathon time may like to continue with the above schedule but make the following adjustments:

- Between weeks 3 and 10, increase the number of consecutive training days from 5 up to 6 by including some extra steady runs that include threshold intervals. This is good speed/distance training but will depend on your individual fitness. Always taper off in weeks 11 and 12.

- Complete your steady runs and threshold sessions using a course that is undulating. This is important if your target race contains some hilly sections.

A good half marathon time is a great basis for taking the quantum leap into full marathon training. Many runners stop at the half marathon distance, but for those runners who are up for the challenge, Chapter 7 uses a sustained half marathon performance as a basis for developing into the full marathon distance. Many marathon runners use their half marathon time as a way of gauging what their potential full marathon performance might be. This is a good place to start.

References

1 Grubb, H. (2011)
   WMA Age-grading calculator 2006 (updated 2010)
   http://www.howardgrubb.co.uk/athletics/wmalookup06.html

2 Riegel, P. (1977)
   Runners World Race Time Predictor
   http://www.runnersworld.co.uk/general/rws-race-time-predictor/1681.html

Chapter 7

Full Marathon Training

The following chapter outlines two 15-week example marathon training schedules that take a sustained half marathon performance as a baseline for running a full marathon non-stop. There is no doubt that full marathon running is one of the more tougher sporting challenges, but the potential for success is phenomenal if we approach things in a way that is both structured and consistent.

The two example schedules are based on an expected weekly mileage of 25-40 miles (Schedule 1), and 40-55 miles (Schedule 2). In the same way as in Chapter 6, you can decide which of the schedules best fits your ability based on your current weekly mileage and fitness level.

What does it take to run a good marathon non-stop?
There are three things that aspiring marathon runners need to pay close attention too as far as their training endeavours are concerned:

I. Mental preparation and mind-set – Training for a marathon and completing the race in a good finish time is not easy – even the winner of a marathon event will tell us that, despite how easy they make it look. When the going gets tough, a healthy dose of determination will train our mind and body to continually push the *wall* back towards the Finish line. "I am because of my mind", is a well known remark made by Paavo Nurmi (Finnish Long Distance Runner) and is highly relevant to a marathon race, particularly in the latter stages. Psychological strength is a critical part of being successful in marathon running and is something that we develop through regular training.

II. Commitment and focus – Completing a 15-week training plan requires tremendous amounts of commitment and focus plus the ability to ignore feelings of doubt and other everyday noise. Without commitment and focus, training sessions get missed and plans can go awry. This often happens because of unavoidable reasons such as general lifestyle issues such as work and family commitments.

III. Training – In marathon running, you need to know what you are doing and why. Some of the most successful people are those who have understood the basics of a particular sphere of knowledge and have then learnt how to apply the principles well – that tends to be their starting point in all that they do, and much of this is down to their training. Your body can take up to two years to fully adapt before you reach your marathon performance peak. The example training schedules in this chapter will provide structure, consistency and regularity to help the body adapt to a higher level of aerobic ability and physical strength ideal for marathon running.

What are the common pitfalls that marathon runners make?
A large part of being successful in marathon running is about race preparation, developing race pace and the mastery of nutrition and hydration. The following examples summarise many of the pitfalls made by marathoners, but also represent some of the underlying reasons why many marathoners don't improve their finish times above and beyond a certain point:

I. Arriving at the start feeling tired – This is not a great start to a competition. If you are feeling tired on the start line of a marathon race then who knows what you will feel like at the finish.

II. Over-training – Training beyond our physical and aerobic limitations leads to fatigue and exhaustion. This will make us more prone to injury and serve to limit the amount of energy available for the race itself.

III. A failure to taper-off correctly – You must complete all of your longer runs at least 3 weeks before race day as any further endurance activity will not benefit your aerobic capacity in any significant way. Unfortunately, some runners sneak a *panic* long run during a tapering off period. This will drain much needed energy resources that are best kept for race day.

IV. Completing the first half of the race too quickly – When we set out too quickly, we run the risk of consuming too much energy in the first half of the race, and then suffering from exhaustion, glycogen-depletion and dehydration in the second half. Some runners perform in a marathon race as if they were doing a half marathon. They achieve a great time at the halfway mark, but as they approach the 18 mile mark, feelings of tiredness set in and their speed starts to drop. Come the last 6 miles or so, they will probably be walking and running, albeit with tired legs, unable to really get going again. We avoid these kinds of situations by developing a sustainable race pace – more on this later.

MARATHON RACE PREPARATION

Success in marathon training requires excellent and precise preparation. This section considers a number of critical training areas that will require a significant amount of focus.

Making the transition to the full marathon distance

The incremental training effort required to run a full marathon is more than twice the amount required for a half marathon. A good way of building up to the full marathon distance is to use the 16 or 20 mile race events as *training runs* and see how you get on. This way of training provides some good exposure to the kinds of physical and mental experiences that await you in a 15-week full marathon training schedule, and just as importantly, the marathon race itself. Be careful though if you choose to actually *race* a 16 or 20 mile distance during a period of marathon training as these distances can zap energy that is required for other quality trainings like speed sessions. A better use of a 16 or 20 mile race is to use them *as* training runs.

The six training practices revisited

Chapter 4 introduced six different types of running training practice aimed at developing performance and endurance. They are all highly relevant to marathon training. Runners may wish to revisit some of the material before progressing any further in this chapter:

I. Recovery (pages 73–75) – Weekly recovery runs are included in both of the schedules. These are best completed on the Monday after a Sunday long run to ensure an adequate recovery in time for any speed sessions scheduled for any weekdays. Recovery is another measure of general fitness, but like other aspects of training, we get better at it through regular practice. As you progress in marathon training, it is likely that you will recover much quicker and be more than ready for the next harder training session.

II. Speed (pages 75–82) – *VO2 Max* and *Threshold* training sessions are included throughout the schedules. The ongoing and continual development of your individual speed through VO2 Max and threshold training is one of the most important factors that will get you to the finish line quicker. When we then add speed training to our base mileage runs and develop our marathon race pace, we achieve the best possible combination of achieving a PB.

III. Hills (pages 82–86) – A number of hill training sessions are included in the schedules that complement the VO2 Max and Threshold speed related sessions. Hill training is an important part of developing the required stamina and strength to run a good marathon. For undulating and hilly marathons, you can choose to combine hill training with a speed related session.

IV. Long runs (pages 86–89) – Long runs and the subsequent development of base mileage is the single most important part of marathon training. Without base mileage, it would be difficult to run 26.2 miles non-stop. There are *three* 20-mile long runs scheduled for weeks 7, 9 and 12. It is very important to do these.

Long runs are a critical part of our *mitochondria* development, the part of our muscles where aerobic energy is created. As we develop our muscles and muscle strength, we will start to burn fat more efficiently as a result.

Long runs should be done at a pace that is 15-20% slower than your marathon race pace as per the guidelines from Chapter 4 (pages 87–88). Base mileage development during the early part of the schedules is done at a comfortable pace. From Week 9 and onwards, you will need to run *part* of your Sunday long run at your marathon race pace.

V. Race pace (pages 89–90) – Race pace practice begins as part of the Sunday long runs as an initial one-off from Week 3, and then more regularly from Week 9 onwards. The development and practice of marathon race pace is sometimes the difference between a PB and disappointment on race day. Speed and base mileage development, regular recovery and rest days, plus correct nutrition and hydration are all worthless pursuits in the absence of race pace if you are planning on running a fast marathon. The body will deliver a stronger aerobic and physical output when we run at a consistent pace over a sustained distance.

Running at a consistent pace will utilise our fat and carbohydrate energy resources far more efficiently. If we were to run each mile at a pace 5-10 seconds *faster* than our trained race pace, then this will have an adverse impact on our performance during the second half of the race, a situation that we must avoid.

In the two example schedules, you will be encouraged to practice your marathon race pace as an integral part of your longer runs (Week 9 and onwards). Before then, you will need to gauge your expected marathon finish time so that you can then gauge your marathon pace and start your race pace training as you mean to go on. Our target marathon pace can be gauged and calculated using Pete Riegel's race performance formula[1] as follows:

$$T2 \text{ (full marathon time)} = T1 \times (D2/D1) \text{ ^ } 1.06$$

Where:

T1 = completion time of a previous race (in minutes)
D1 = distance of a previous race
T2 = calculated expected time of the target race (in minutes)
D2 = distance of the target race
^ = the *caret* symbol and signifies exponentiation
1.06 = a constant value that applies to all uses of the formula

Let us assume that you have followed the schedules from Chapter 6 and have achieved a half marathon time of 1:40 (100 minutes). Using the formula above, an expected full marathon time (i.e. T2) could be:

$$T2 \text{ (full marathon time)} = 100 \times (26.2/13.1) \text{ ^ } 1.06 = 208.5 \text{ minutes}$$

A T2 value of 208.5 minutes equates to a full marathon time of 3:28:30.

Therefore, to achieve a marathon time of 3:28:30, you would need to maintain a pace of just under 8-minute miles (or 7:57 to be absolutely precise).

Be aware that a time of 3:28:30 is an estimate. If you have never previously run further than 13.1 miles then it will take time to develop your base mileage, threshold pace, core fitness and race pace, and not to mention skills in nutrition and hydration before clocking 3:28:30 at the finish line. Given that regular race pace intervals will be a part of your long runs, you will still have some time to fully gauge whether or not your target marathon race pace is going to be sustainable. It is important to be disciplined and practice your target race pace in the longer runs as instructed. If you struggle to maintain a particular pace then it might be worth readjusting your performance expectations. Please don't be despondent – there is always next time. You will just need to continue to develop a solid base mileage and remain focused on speed training. Then as time progresses, your body will adapt and condition itself for marathon training. By taking this approach, you will also help prevent unnecessary injury through over-training.

VI. Rest (pages 90–92) – When we take regular rest periods, we give our body time to adapt to a higher level of aerobic ability. As we move into marathon running, the amount of rest that we get on a weekly basis will reduce. By the time that you have progressed through the training schedules in Chapter 6 then you should be able to train at varying levels of distance and intensity for around 4-5 days on the trot (full marathon training is about 5-6 consecutive days of training in any single week).

Cross training and core fitness
We have already learnt a number of times in previous chapters how important it is to develop an upright posture for running. The development of a strong core is a critical part of marathon conditioning. From Week 2, the long runs will get progressively longer and this may cause our body to slouch during the latter stages of a longer run, a situation that often happens as a result of

general tiredness and one that will have an adverse effect on our overall running performance. Slouching during running practice is reduced when we maintain a strong core and develop a more upright posture.

Weekly sessions of cross training and core fitness are included in Schedule 1 up to week 13. In Schedule 2, these sessions have been replaced with an extra weekly run to cater for the increase in overall weekly mileage, whilst at the same time still allowing for at least one rest day. The inclusion of extra-curricular sports in Schedule 2 is therefore a matter of individual choice where it is possible to replace one of the weekday runs or perhaps the occasional rest day with a (e.g.) weekly circuits' session. Nevertheless, it is important to remember that at least 80% of your marathon training throughout the 15 weeks should still be running related.

Nutrition and Hydration for marathon training

Nutrition and Hydration were covered in Chapter 3 where we considered the areas of *Food Diet*, *Training Nutrition* and *Fluid Intake and Hydration*. Readers may wish to recap on the content before going any further as it is highly relevant to marathon training.

In marathon running, there are two critical situations that we need to avoid if we are to run 26.2 miles non-stop. They are *glycogen-depletion* and *dehydration*. Glycogen-depletion is prevented through adequate carbohydrate consumption. Dehydration is avoided through adequate water consumption. Let us take a look at each one in the context of marathon running:

I. Carbohydrate consumption – Glycogen-depletion is synonymous with hitting the *wall* and is a situation that we can avoid if we fuel our body correctly. If you have been previously led to believe that hitting the wall during a marathon race is a foregone conclusion (typically around the 18-20 mile mark), then the following sections should help to put your mind at rest. We maintain our glycogen stocks in two ways: *Pre-carb loading* and *Glycogen replenishment*.

A. Pre-carb loading (Chapter 3 pages 42–45) is concerned with how much carbohydrate we consume before training. The training schedules that follow later in the chapter will require at least 6 days a week of training, with varying combinations of high intensity and distance training with at least one rest day. The schedules also assume that you are planning on running a fast marathon, i.e. at a pace anywhere between 75-80% MHR.

To cope with this volume of training, you will need to include a regular supply of carbohydrates in your weekly food diet so that your body has a regular access to an efficient source of fast energy. During the week (from around Monday to Thursday) you should consume around 5-7g of carbohydrate per Kg of body weight. This should be sufficient for the purposes of shorter but high-intensity training. During the latter part of the week, and in the run up to a longer run of around (e.g.) 2-3 hours scheduled for a Sunday, you should consume around 8-10g of carbohydrate per Kg of body weight, or thereabouts.

Some runners may need to train their body over a period of time to consume carbohydrates particularly for longer runs. As you progress into your longer runs, you will condition your body to preserve carbohydrates and burn fat more efficiently. As a result, your carbohydrate stocks will last for longer and help prevent glycogen-depletion.

B. Glycogen replenishment (page 50) is the practice of topping-up our glycogen stocks *during* training. This is critical for those runners who cannot consume an adequate quantity of carbohydrates for the full duration of a long training run. Glycogen-depletion is known to happen very quickly and it is important to identify the signs early during a training run, a lack of concentration in the mind being one known symptom. Energy drinks and gels are useful for the purposes of glycogen replenishment as they provide good sources of glucose that are easily consumed and absorbed during training. Given their high sugar content, they should also be taken with some water. Acquiring a waist band for carrying gels and/or an energy drink during training is a good idea. Your local running specialist will be able to help here.

What kinds of energy products are there?
As discussed previously in Chapter 3 (pages 49–52), there are many energy drinks and gels available; your local running specialist will have an assortment to choose from. In terms of what to use on race

day, you have two choices: either you can use your own energy drink and carry it with you during the race, or alternatively, find out which energy product the race organisers are going to provide on race day and do your marathon training using that one.

Example refuelling strategy
During any typical training week, and in the days preceding a long run, you will need to work out your individual carbohydrate requirements using the simple pre-carb loading and glycogen replenishment metrics mentioned earlier, and previously in Chapter 3. Once you know this, you will then need to calculate how many gels or how much energy drink you will need to carry with you during the run for the purposes of replenishment. Then during training, glycogen replenishment becomes a case of *how-much how-often*. If you are new to marathon running and are not used to doing long runs then you may need to start replenishing early in the run, e.g. from around 60-90 minutes into a 2-hour run. You could start by taking 2 gels with you during your training run and take one every half an hour. As you become more used to doing longer runs and perhaps be able to pre-load carbohydrates more efficiently, you may then start to utilise carbohydrate and fat more efficiently and as a result start replenishing glycogen stocks a little later in the training run. This is all down to practice and what works for the individual.

II. Rehydration – Dehydration when running is largely avoided by understanding our individual hydration cycles, and this will come through regular practice. Generally speaking, if during training you *think* that you are thirsty then you probably *are* thirsty and therefore need to take on further water. You will only have a short time of between 15-20 minutes to consume some water before the tipping point occurs and dehydration starts to set in. Recovering from dehydration when running is very difficult because the body can only consume comparatively small amounts of water in any single dose (100-150ml) without causing stomach cramps and bloatedness. Dehydration is avoided by sipping water regularly rather than through a large amount of fluid in one go (before, during and after training). We should aim to consume a minimum of 2 litres of water per day as a baseline requirement. The amount of water that we would consume during a training run is derived from the amount of body weight that was lost during a training run. On a warmer day we may need to consume as much as 50% more fluid. Rehydration in marathon running is best started within the first 30-60 minutes of a training run with the regular sipping of around 100-150ml of water (a small cupful) at any one time – any quantity larger than this may result in stomach cramps.

On the flip side, we should also avoid over-hydration (or *hypotranemia* – page 54). Over-hydration can cause two situations to ccur. Firstly, the body will reject the excess fluid. Persistently having to stop and discharge body fluids during a race is both inconvenient and unnecessary. Secondly, it reduces the concentration of sodium in the blood, a chemical that helps *digest* and *retain* fluid. Given the growing popularity of marathon running and the obvious hysteria that goes with dehydration, many marathon runners incorrectly over-consume with water. The best way of avoiding these kinds of situations is to use an energy drink that contains sodium, and only consume enough water to replace what was lost during training.

Tapering off

The tapering off period in marathon training begins about 3 weeks prior to race day, which is normally the week after your last 20 mile training run (*Stage 3* of the training schedules). During tapering-off, you should reduce your running distance and rest more often, but keep your training intensity high with shorter bursts of speed training. It is important to preserve as much of your energy for race day. You will not gain any significant advantage by doing further longer runs during the tapering off period. Avoid doing any significant amounts of cross training or trying anything new training-wise. If you need a new pair of running shoes in advance of race day, then purchase these at about Week 7, or thereabouts.

It is important to start preparing your kit bag about 3-4 days prior to race day. For a Sunday marathon, try and get a good night's sleep on the Thursday and Friday before race day. Early start races may require you to practice an earlier than usual breakfast routine, and so be sure to include this in your training.

Race and race day Strategy

The formulation of an effective race strategy is a critical part of race execution. It is critical to never deviate on race day from how you have trained. Why would you do something completely different on race day? It is those runners who stick to how they have trained and ignore all the marathon euphoria going on in the background that increase their chances of crossing the finish line with a PB. There are three areas that will require focused attention: *Travel to the venue*, *Pre-race warm-up* and *Race strategy*:

I. Travel to venue – Getting to the start of a race will depend on the event as some events like (e.g.) the London Marathon have the start and finish areas in different locations. For the Boston and New York marathons, the organisers will transport you out to the start area, whereas the Chicago Marathon has the start and finish areas positioned back to back. Nevertheless, it is good to arrive at the start at least 90 minutes before the race is due to begin. This gives you enough time to prepare, visit the facilities and take a 40-minute rest before making your way to the baggage and start areas.

II. Pre-race warm-up – Your pre-race warm-up routine is likely to be a gentle jog to the start area plus a few gentle stretches when waiting in the starting pens. When the start gun sounds, you are ready to go straight away.

III. Race strategy – When we think about how we could execute a marathon race on race day and perform well as a result, it is good to split the race into several stages. This book suggests splitting the 26.2 mile course into *four* stages:

Stage 1 is the first 1-3 miles. Many marathoners take the first few miles or so of a race gently. This will help relax the mind and get into the race. For the big races, the competitors may take a little time to thin out, but come the end of this stage the course should be less crowded. Some marathoners might be concerned that this approach may reduce their overall time. Race PBs are gained or lost in the second half and so starting out in the race a little slowly shouldn't therefore pose a major problem.

Stage 2 is up to the halfway mark (13.1 miles). Runners should already know roughly what their halfway time should be. For example, if your *half marathon* time is 1:35 and your trained marathon pace is 8-minute miles then your halfway time should be around 1:43, assuming an even-pace. If you get there sooner, you may have gone out too quickly and will need to be very careful as you go into Stage 3. If you are a little past that time, then you need to gauge things at the 18-20 mile mark and see how you feel. It is generally considered safer to be a little late to the halfway mark than it is to be early. It really depends on how you feel and whether or not you are running at a sustained pace. This is another reason why race pace development in training is so important. Remember that there is no such thing as *time in the bank*. Having 5 minutes in the bank for the second half because of an over-performance in the first half is a luxury that rarely leads to anything. You will probably lose twice that amount in time per mile in the second half. This is a scenario that is best avoided.

Stage 3 is from the halfway mark to the 18-20 mile mark. It is important to keep taking on water and maintaining your glycogen levels. If you are going to dehydrate or get low on energy, this is the stage in the race when it will probably happen. The 18-20 mile mark is a well known part of the race where runners can hit the *wall* and then struggle in Stage 4. We can avoid this scenario and push the wall closer to the finish if we master race nutrition and keep running at the pace we trained at.

Stage 4 is the last 6 miles or so. They say that a marathon race starts at 20 miles – this is the psychological halfway mark. Much of the training that you have been doing is geared towards surviving the last 6.2 miles or so. It is when things start to get tough – "Anyone can run 20 miles. It's the next 6 that count", Barry Magee, New Zealand Athlete (Ret.). If you started the race gently and took the first half at the pace at which you trained, and you get to 20 miles still feeling strong then that PB could be yours. The key thing now is focus, determination and the refusal to give in. You will have the crowds on your side and you may also have time on your side simply because you have kept your critical reserves for the last half of the race. Keep taking on water and gauging your glycogen levels and push that wall back to the finish line as far as it will go.

Post-Race training

Recovery from a marathon race is an important part of getting back into training. After a marathon race, you should aim to take a few days off from exercise before getting back into doing any training. Individual recovery times can vary, but most marathoners stay away from high-intensity and long distance running for about 2-3 weeks after the race (about 1 day of recovery for every mile raced is a well known recovery measure). Within a few days of completing a marathon, start gently moving again by doing some short easy runs during the first few weeks coupled with the usual pre and post-training stretches. Many marathoners often do some cross training as a way of switching off from running altogether.

FULL MARATHON TRAINING SCHEDULES

We are now in a position to start working on the two example 15-week-marathon schedules. Schedule 1 is based on a plan that helped me achieve a marathon time of between 3:30 and 4 hours. Schedule 2 is an enhancement to Schedule 1 that helped me achieve a time of sub 3:30. Runners can choose which of the two schedules best fits their experience level and current weekly mileage.

Training Schedule	Experience level
Schedule 1: Full Marathon 25-40 miles/week	Sub 2-hour Half Marathon/20 miles running per week including one continuous long run of at least 10 miles
Schedule 2: Full Marathon 40-55 miles/week	Sub 1:40 Half Marathon/30 miles running per week including one continuous long run of at least 15 miles

Notes and guidelines for the schedules

The following example marathon schedules below are structured into three discrete parts covering the full 15 weeks of training: *Endurance* (weeks 1-5), *Speed and Endurance* (weeks 6-12) and *Tapering Off* (weeks 13-15). The same four principles of *Endurance and stamina*, *Speed*, *Recovery and rest* and *Race pace* from Chapter 6 are also used in this chapter as well.

The training schedules will require practice and perseverance. Marathon running is not easy and you should not feel despondent if your first attempt at the distance falls short of your aspirations. If you find any part of the schedules too difficult, then cut back the intensity to a more manageable level.

Try to avoid missing the long runs – these are important for developing base mileage. This is the part of the training regime that will *get you round*. If you don't get a chance to do the speed sessions then these can be developed in the future.

The basic idea around both of the schedules is to develop strength and speed whilst building base mileage up to 20 miles. Both schedules have two low intensity weeks (weeks 5 and 8) that allow for a few quiet periods in between the core periods of high intensity training before tapering off in advance of race day.

SCHEDULE 1: Full Marathon 25-40 miles/week
The following 15-week training plan is aimed at someone who can run at least 20 miles a week that includes a continuous 10 mile run, and has achieved a sustained and consistent half marathon time of sub 2 hours.

Stage 1: Endurance (weeks 1-5)
A summary of the four training categories is as follows:

Endurance and stamina – Build an initial level of endurance by developing long run mileage from 8 to 15 miles by Week 4. Regular cross training is encouraged from Week 3 onwards.

Speed – One weekly speed session is scheduled that is either Threshold, VO2 Max or Hills.

Recovery and rest – Two rest days are allowed in weeks 1 and 2 but is reduced to a single rest day for weeks 3 and 4 as training mileage and intensity is increased. Week 5 is the first of two low intensity weeks consisting of a reduced distance and training intensity.

Race pace – Race pace practice as part of the Sunday long runs begins from Week 9 in Stage 2. For now, concentrate on building base mileage and speed.

SCHEDULE 1: 25-40 miles/week	
Stage 1 weeks 1-5	
WEEK 1	
Monday	4 miles Easy
Tuesday	3 x 7 minutes @ threshold pace 3 minutes recovery between each threshold
Wednesday	Rest
Thursday	4 miles Steady
Friday	Rest
Saturday	4 miles Easy
Sunday	8 miles
WEEK 2	
Monday	4 miles Easy
Tuesday	3 sets of 8-minute hill reps 3-minute recovery between each set
Wednesday	Rest
Thursday	4 miles Steady
Friday	Rest
Saturday	4 miles Easy
Sunday	10 miles
WEEK 3	
Monday	4 miles Easy
Tuesday	Cross training or core fitness
Wednesday	5 miles Steady
Thursday	7 miles Steady Include 6 x 100m @ 5K pace with 100m Easy
Friday	Rest
Saturday	4 miles Easy
Sunday	12 miles
WEEK 4	
Monday	4 miles Easy
Tuesday	3 x 10 minutes @ threshold pace 2-minute recovery between each threshold
Wednesday	4 miles Easy

continued...

Thursday	Cross training or core fitness
Friday	Rest
Saturday	5 miles Easy
Sunday	15 miles
WEEK 5	
Monday	4 miles Easy
Tuesday	5 miles Steady Include 6 x 200m @ 5K pace with 200m Easy
Wednesday	Rest
Thursday	Cross training or core fitness
Friday	Rest
Saturday	5 miles Easy
Sunday	10 miles

Stage 2: Speed and Endurance (weeks 6-12)

A summary of the four training categories is as follows:

Endurance and stamina – Three 20 mile runs are scheduled for weeks 7, 9 and 12 with shorter runs on weekdays. The 20 milers form a critical part of developing base mileage and should not be missed. From Week 9, the amount of consecutive training days increases from 5 days to 6 days and then 7 days by weeks 12/13.

Speed – Two speed sessions are scheduled during weeks 7, 9, 10 and 12 using a combination of VO2 Max, Threshold and Hills. Weeks 6, 8 and 11 have just a single speed session.

Recovery and rest – Week 8 is the last of the two low intensity weeks and follows the first of the three 20 mile long runs. The number of rest days will reduce from 2 days down to 1 day from Week 9 onwards with 7 days of consecutive training scheduled for weeks 12 and into 13.

Race pace – From Week 9, most of the Sunday long runs will include varying elements of marathon race pace practice. This is a critical part of marathon training. During this stage you will need to be absolutely sure that your chosen marathon pace is sustainable. Make any amendments as required.

Stage 2 schedule (weeks 6-12)	
WEEK 6	
Monday	4 miles Easy
Tuesday	3 sets of 8-minute hill reps 2-minute recovery between each set
Wednesday	4 miles Easy
Thursday	Cross training or core fitness
Friday	Rest
Saturday	4 miles Easy
Sunday	15 miles
WEEK 7	
Monday	4 miles Easy
Tuesday	6 miles Steady Include 6 x 400m @ 5K pace with 200m Easy
Wednesday	Cross training or core fitness
Thursday	Rest
Friday	3x10 minutes @ threshold pace 3-minute recovery between each threshold
Saturday	4 miles Easy
Sunday	20 miles
WEEK 8	
Monday	Rest
Tuesday	5 miles Steady
Wednesday	3 sets of 7-minute hill reps 2-minute recovery between each set
Thursday	Cross training or core fitness
Friday	Rest
Saturday	4 miles Easy
Sunday	13 miles
WEEK 9	
Monday	4 miles Easy
Tuesday	5 miles Steady Include 6 x 400m @ 5K pace with 200m Easy
Wednesday	Rest
Thursday	2 x 11 minutes @ threshold pace 3-minute recovery between each threshold
Friday	Rest

continued...

Saturday	4 miles Easy
Sunday	20 miles – miles 7 to 14 @ Marathon pace
WEEK 10	
Monday	4 miles Easy
Tuesday	3 sets of 8-minute hill reps 3-minute recovery between each set
Wednesday	Cross training or core fitness
Thursday	Rest
Friday	7 miles Steady Include 6 x 400m @ 5K pace with 200m Easy
Saturday	4 miles Easy
Sunday	17 miles
WEEK 11	
Monday	4 miles Easy
Tuesday	7 miles Steady
Wednesday	Rest
Thursday	6 miles Steady Include 6 x 400m @ 5K pace with 200m Easy
Friday	Cross training or core fitness
Saturday	5 miles Easy
Sunday	18 miles – last 9 miles @ Marathon pace
WEEK 12	
Monday	4 miles Easy
Tuesday	5 miles Steady Include 6 x 400m @ 5K pace with 200m Easy
Wednesday	Rest
Thursday	2 x 15 minutes @ threshold pace 3-minute recovery between each threshold
Friday	Cross training or core fitness
Saturday	4 miles Easy
Sunday	20 miles – miles 5 to 15 @ Marathon pace

Stage 3: Taper Off (weeks 13-15)

A summary of the four training categories is as follows:

Endurance and stamina – Weekly mileage is significantly reduced in the run-up to race day. Extended longer runs will serve very little purpose at this stage of marathon training and should therefore be avoided. If for any reason you haven't managed to complete your three 20 milers then it might be worth reducing your target race pace to ensure that you preserve as much energy as is possible during the race.

Speed – During this stage, it is important to keep the training intensity level high but only in short intervals. There are a number of shorter VO2 Max and Threshold sessions scheduled during the tapering off period that help keep the *fast-twitch* muscles well-conditioned in time for race day.

Recovery and rest – The number of weekly rest days is increased to around 2 days during tapering-off. This might seem low, but one of the aims of this stage is to still train nearly as *frequently*, but with a reduced *quantity* of training.

Race pace – By now you should know what your expected marathon pace is going to be, having practiced it a number of times during the longer runs in Stage 2. This will continue in weeks 13 and 14. You will then have one more training run in the early part of race week that includes an element of marathon pace that will serve as a quick reminder in time for race day.

Stage 3 schedule (weeks 13-15)	
WEEK 13	
Monday	4 miles Easy
Tuesday	3 x 8 minutes @ threshold pace 3-minute recovery between each threshold
Wednesday	4 miles Easy
Thursday	Rest
Friday	4 miles Easy
Saturday	Cross training or core fitness
Sunday	13 miles – last 5 miles @ Marathon pace

WEEK 14	
Monday	4 miles Easy
Tuesday	5 miles Steady Include 6 x 200m @ 5K pace with 100m Easy
Wednesday	Rest
Thursday	3 x 6 minutes @ threshold pace 3-minute recovery between each threshold
Friday	4 miles Easy
Saturday	Rest
Sunday	9 miles – miles 4 to 8 @ Marathon pace
WEEK 15 – Race Week	
Monday	Rest
Tuesday	4 miles Easy
Wednesday	5 miles – last 2 miles @ Marathon pace
Thursday	Rest
Friday	4 miles – 5 x 100m sprints 200m Easy in second half
Saturday	4 miles Easy
Sunday	RACE DAY

SCHEDULE 2: Full Marathon 40-55 miles/week

The second of the two 15-week training plans is aimed at someone who can run at least 30 miles a week that includes a continuous 15 mile run, and has achieved a sustained and consistent half marathon time of under 1:40. Schedule 2 is an extended follow-on from Schedule 1 and emphasises an increase in weekly mileage and speed training as a way of further developing marathon performance. The long run training distances remains very similar with runners still being expected to complete *three* 20 mile long runs. The amount of rest days also remains very much the same. The main differences fall into two areas:

I. The addition of a second weekly run – The weekly cross training and core fitness sessions have been replaced with a second weekly run of a distance between 6 and 8 miles. This will increase the total weekly mileage by around 35%. If you want to include some extra-curricular sporting activity in this schedule then you can either replace a weekday run or an occasional rest day with some non-running related sporting activity. Nevertheless, at least 80% of your marathon training throughout the 15 weeks should still be running related.

II. Longer speed training sessions – This will increase by around 35% but will use the same recovery period times as in Schedule 1. The main aim here is to do longer speed sessions as a way of developing further speed over a sustained distance.

SCHEDULE 2: 40-55 miles/week	
Stage 1 schedule (weeks 1-5)	
WEEK 1	
Monday	5 miles Easy
Tuesday	3 x 10 minutes @ threshold pace 3-minute recovery between each threshold
Wednesday	Rest
Thursday	8 miles Steady
Friday	Rest
Saturday	5 miles Easy
Sunday	9 miles
WEEK 2	
Monday	5 miles Easy
Tuesday	3 sets of 12-minute hill reps 3-minute recovery between each set
Wednesday	Rest
Thursday	8 miles Steady
Friday	Rest
Saturday	5 miles Easy
Sunday	12 miles
WEEK 3	
Monday	5 miles Easy
Tuesday	7 miles Steady
Wednesday	4 miles Easy
Thursday	8 miles Steady Include 8 x 100m @ 5K pace with 100m Easy
Friday	Rest
Saturday	5 miles Easy
Sunday	14 miles

WEEK 4	
Monday	5 miles Easy
Tuesday	3 x 13 minutes @ threshold pace 2-minute recovery between each threshold
Wednesday	5 miles Easy
Thursday	8 miles Steady
Friday	Rest
Saturday	5 miles Easy
Sunday	16 miles
WEEK 5	
Monday	4 miles Easy
Tuesday	6 miles Steady Include 8 x 200m @ 5K pace with 200m Easy
Wednesday	4 miles Easy
Thursday	6 miles Steady
Friday	Rest
Saturday	4 miles Easy
Sunday	9 miles
Stage 2 schedule (weeks 6-12)	
WEEK 6	
Monday	5 miles Easy
Tuesday	3 sets of 12-minute hill reps 2-minute recovery between each set
Wednesday	4 miles Easy
Thursday	8 miles Steady
Friday	Rest
Saturday	5 miles Easy
Sunday	14 miles
WEEK 7	
Monday	5 miles Easy
Tuesday	7 miles Steady Include 8 x 400m @ 5K pace with 200m Easy
Wednesday	8 miles Steady
Thursday	Rest
Friday	3 x 13 minutes @ threshold pace 3-minute recovery between each threshold
Saturday	5 miles Easy
Sunday	20 miles

WEEK 8	
Monday	Rest
Tuesday	7 miles Steady
Wednesday	3 sets of 10-minute hill reps 2-minute recovery between each set
Thursday	4 miles Easy
Friday	Rest
Saturday	5 miles Easy
Sunday	13 miles

WEEK 9	
Monday	5 miles Easy
Tuesday	6 miles Steady Include 8 x 400m @ 5K pace with 200m Easy
Wednesday	Rest
Thursday	2 x 15 minutes @ threshold 3-minute recovery between each threshold
Friday	8 miles Steady
Saturday	5 miles Easy
Sunday	20 miles – miles 7 to 14 @ Marathon pace

WEEK 10	
Monday	5 miles Easy
Tuesday	7 miles Steady
Wednesday	3 sets of 12-minute hill reps 3-minute recovery between each set
Thursday	Rest
Friday	7 miles Steady Include 8 x 400m @ 5K pace with 200m Easy
Saturday	5 miles Easy
Sunday	18 miles

WEEK 11	
Monday	5 miles Easy
Tuesday	7 miles Steady
Wednesday	Rest
Thursday	8 miles Steady Include 8 x 400m @ 5K pace with 200m Easy
Friday	10 miles Steady
Saturday	5 miles Easy
Sunday	18 miles – last 9 miles @ Marathon pace

WEEK 12	
Monday	5 miles Easy
Tuesday	8 miles Steady Include 8 x 400m @ 5K pace with 200m Easy
Wednesday	Rest
Thursday	2 x 15 minutes @ threshold pace 3-minute recovery between each threshold
Friday	6 miles Steady
Saturday	4 miles Easy
Sunday	20 miles – miles 5 to 15 @ Marathon pace

Stage 3 schedule (weeks 13-15)

WEEK 13	
Monday	4 miles Easy
Tuesday	4 x 8 minutes @ threshold pace 3-minute recovery between each threshold
Wednesday	6 miles Easy
Thursday	Rest
Friday	6 miles Steady
Saturday	5 miles Easy
Sunday	14 miles – last 6 miles @ Marathon pace

WEEK 14	
Monday	5 miles Easy
Tuesday	6 miles Steady Include 8 x 200m @ 5K pace with 100m Easy
Wednesday	Rest
Thursday	4x6 minutes @ threshold pace 3-minute recovery between each threshold
Friday	5 miles Easy
Saturday	Rest
Sunday	10 miles – miles 4 to 8 @ Marathon pace

WEEK 15 – Race Week	
Monday	Rest
Tuesday	5 miles Easy
Wednesday	7 miles – last 2 miles @ Marathon pace
Thursday	Rest
Friday	5 miles – 5 x 100m sprints 200m Easy in second half
Saturday	4 miles Easy
Sunday	RACE DAY

Further reading on marathon running

For any readers who are looking at taking their marathon training to the next level, *Advanced Marathoning* by Pete Pfitzinger and Scott Douglas (Human Kinetics, 2009) is an excellent book that builds on many of the ideas around further endurance training and lactate threshold. Once you have got to a point in your own marathon development where you are comfortable doing Level 3 Speed and Hill sessions (Chapter 4), and have mastered the marathon training content in Schedule 2 and have a half marathon time that is getting close to sub 1:30, then you may stand to benefit from the more advanced training concepts outlined by Pfitzinger and Douglas.

References

1 Riegel, P. (1977)
Runners World Race Time Predictor
http://www.runnersworld.co.uk/general/rws-race-time-predictor/1681.html

Glossary

The following terms and abbreviations are used throughout this book.

Aerobic Capacity	The total amount of oxygen that is consumed during aerobic exercise.
Aerobic Exercise	Physical exercise that depends primarily on using oxygen as a means of generating energy.
Aerobic Improvement	The process of enhancing the body's ability to generate energy from oxygen.
Anaerobic training	Very fast aerobic training that causes the body to produce more lactate than what it is capable of processing
Blood Pressure	The pressure of the blood that circulates around the body and relates to the force and rate of the heartbeat as well as the diameter and elasticity of the arterial walls.
Body Composition	Concerned with the percentages of fat, bone, water and muscle in a human body.
Body Fat Percentage	The proportion of our body weight that is made up of fat (expressed as a percentage).
Body Mass Index (BMI)	A simple but inaccurate index of weight-for-height that is used to classify the weight of adults.
Body Weight	The total weight of our body measured in Pounds (lb) or Kilogram's (Kg)
Carbohydrate loading	The process of stocking up on carbohydrate foods in advance of high intensity or endurance training.
Carbohydrates – Complex	Carbohydrate foods that take longer to digest but contain good sources of longer term energy storage in the form of glycogen.
Carbohydrates – Simple	Foods that contain high levels of sugar and starch that digest easily but cause spikes in blood sugar levels.
Cardiovascular	Relating to the heart and the blood vessels.
Cool-down	The process of gently allowing the body to return to normal after a training session.
Core Fitness	The development of the abdominal and stomach muscles and associated regions of the body.
Cross Country	Running in rugged and undulating landscape. Normally done in the winter months.

Cross Training	Non-running related sports like Cycling, Swimming.
Dehydration	A situation that occurs when the body becomes low on water reserves and can no longer function correctly.
Easy-paced running	Running at 65-70% MHR, i.e. a pace slightly faster than conversational.
Endurance	The ability for the body to tolerate exercise for extended periods of time without experiencing excess fatigue.
Energy Supplement	A food type or drink taken by a runner for the purposes of replenishment or recovery.
Fartlek	A way of running training where the pace is continually varied.
Fast-twitch muscles	Muscle fibres that are developed as a result of speed training and are capable of producing large amounts of muscle force very quickly.
Fat – as a source of energy	An important source of energy for runners derived from burning either body fat, or from foods that contain fat.
Foot pronation	Used to describe the profile of the foot as it touches the ground when running and will govern the type of shoes required for running.
General Practitioner (GP)	A family doctor, or your first point of contact in the event of any general and everyday medical problems or queries.
Glucagon	A hormone stimulated by proteins that mitigates the fat forming effects of insulin and helps to ensure a stable blood-glucose level.
Glycogen	Energy derived from carbohydrates stored in the muscles for future use.
Glycogen-depletion	A situation that occurs when the body becomes low on glycogen stocks and causes a substantial drop in running performance.
Health and Fitness Assessment	A process of measuring an individual's suitability to running.
Heart-Rate	The number of beats per minute of the heart at any given point in time. This is a measure of pace, or how hard the body is working.
Heart-Rate Monitor	An electronic device worn by a runner during training that measures the heart rate *real-time* and is used to monitor training pace.

Hill Training	Running up a gradient.
Hydration	The process of replenishing the bodies water reserves.
Hyponatremia	An adverse medical condition that occurs when the body becomes over-hydrated and causes a substantial drop in sodium levels.
Injury	Used to describe physical damage to the body
Insulin	A hormone responsible for fat storage in the body
Interval Training	Alternating periods of high and low intensity running training.
Jogging	Running at 60-65% MHR, i.e. a pace than is conversational.
Lactate (or Lactic Acid)	A bi-product of carbohydrate metabolism that is created as a result of doing aerobic exercise.
Long Runs	A training run longer than 60-90 minutes in duration.
Maximum Heart-Rate (MHR)	The largest number of beats per minute that the heart is capable of doing.
Mitochondria	The part of the muscle where aerobic energy is produced.
Nutrition	The area of health concerned with what we eat and drink.
Over-training	The practice of training beyond our physical and aerobic limits.
Oxygen	A component of air that is used to generate aerobic energy.
Pace	Concerned with our heart rate and subsequent speed during running training.
Peak Expiratory Flow	A measure of lung function and capacity.
Post-Race Training	Running training that is done after a race.
Posture	Concerned with the physical position of the body at any one point in time.
Power-walking	Fast walking at a pace of 125% of normal walking speed.
Processed Foods	Foods that have been manufactured or have been through an industrialised process.
Race Day Strategy	The plan of action around how a race will be executed for the purposes of achieving best performance.

Race pace	Concerned with how fast a race will be executed (normally expressed in minute per mile/kilometre).
Recovery	Concerned with how the body returns to a normal state after running training.
Replenishment	The process of feeding the body with food and drink as a result of running training.
Rest	Concerned with taking various amounts of time out from running training.
Resting Pulse Rate	The heart-rate in beats per minute during a period of physical and mental inactivity.
Running Technique	Concerned with the positioning and effective movement of the body during running for the purposes of enhancing performance and endurance.
Slow-twitch Muscles	Muscle fibres that are efficient at using oxygen for extended periods of time and take longer to fatigue. They are developed as a result of doing long runs of 60-90 minutes.
Steady-paced Running	Running at 70-80% MHR, i.e. a pace where you should be able to say one about sentence before being out of breath.
Sweating	Water loss through heat dissipation as a result of doing exercise.
Taper off	A period in the run up to a race where training quantity is reduced in advance of a race day.
Threshold	Running at 80-90% MHR, i.e. a pace where you should be able to say no more than 2-3 words before being out of breath.
VO2 Max	A measure of general aerobic fitness capability.
VO2 Max – Training	Running at 90%+ MHR, i.e. very fast.
Warm-up	The process of increasing the heart rate and body temperature in advance of a training session.
Weight Loss	Concerned with the shedding of body fat and a subsequent reduction in total body fat percentage.

Index

A
Achilles – stretching 33, 59
Active healing 94
Adductors stretch 68
Aerobic capacity 11, 15, 16, 137
Aerobic exercise 2, 13, 17, 74, 81
Age–related race performances
    120–121
Alcohol 13, 46, 55
Anaerobic 15, 81
Arm Back stretch 29

B
Base mileage 86, 87, 96, 119, 124, 127,
    131, 139, 140, 141, 149, 151
Beginners 3, 4, 5, 6, 19, 77, 80, 98, 120,
    124
    courses 7
    training 21–38
Bent knees core exercise 114
Blood pressure 11, 13
Blood–sugar 41, 50, 51
Body composition 11–13
Body fat – percentage 11, 12, 42
    reducing 17–19
Body Hugs stretch 28
Body Mass Index (BMI) 11
Body weight 2, 11, 12, 13, 17, 18, 30,
    42, 43, 44, 53, 62, 76, 92, 143, 145
Breakfast 46, 47, 145
Burpees core exercise 109–110
Butt kicks exercise 27

C
Calf raise stretch 59
Calories 12, 13, 17, 42, 43, 44
Carbohydrates 3, 17, 18, 19, 21, 30,
    39, 45, 46, 47, 48, 49, 50, 51, 55,
    75, 81, 88, 92, 140, 142, 143, 144
    consumption guidelines 42–45
    definition 40-4
    excess 12–13
Cardiovascular 40, 97
Circuit training 98–116
Clothing 22, 30, 72

Coffee 54
Cold weather training 72
Cool–down 30, 62
    stretches 31–34, 63–70
Core fitness 17, 73, 93, 94, 117, 118,
    119, 120, 141, 142, 150, 151, 152,
    153, 154, 155
    overview 95–96
    circuit training 98–116
Cross country 21, 86
Cross training 97–98
Cycling 97

D
Dehydration 30, 41, 51, 53, 138, 144,
    145
    definition 52
    prevention 53, 71, 72, 88, 142
    recovery from 54
Downhill running technique 83

E
Easy–paced running 6, 21, 35, 38, 42,
    75
Endurance 1, 3, 4, 38, 40, 42, 43, 44,
    45, 46, 50, 51, 71, 80, 86, 87, 88,
    95, 97, 117, 124, 127, 131, 137,
    138, 148, 149, 151, 154, 160
Energy bars 47, 48, 50
Energy drink 47, 49, 50, 51, 54, 72,
    143, 144, 145
Energy gels 49, 50, 84, 89, 91, 143, 144
Energy supplements 45, 52, 88
    consumption 49, 50, 51
Evening meal 46, 47, 48

F
Fartlek 76
Fast–twitch muscles 38, 76, 154
Fat 11, 39, 40, 41, 42, 43, 44, 45, 46, 47,
    50, 92, 97, 140
    as a source of energy 42
    burning of 12, 17–19, 47, 87, 139,
    143, 144
    metabolism 13, 42, 44, 87

parkrun – A great introduction to running

In 2004 we saw the birth of *parkrun*, an organisation who arrange free weekly 5K timed runs at various locations around the world where people of all ages and abilities (including Juniors) are encouraged to participate. parkrun events start on a Saturday morning at 09:00 (local time) and attract varying numbers of people each week. At the time of this book going to press, there were over 500 weekly parkrun events being organised across the world with participation continuously on the increase. parkrun represents one of the single most important contributors to encouraging people to take up running.

parkrun

www.parkrun.com
Reprinted with kind permission

Lightning Source UK Ltd.
Milton Keynes UK
UKOW02f2024120915
258511UK00004B/196/P